MW01706675

May 1, 1999

Faith,

Thank you for your support. Keep love & your purpose & your passion alive!

Lovingly
Zelotta
Gospel Radio
1390 AM WGCI
Sundays
5-9 Am

The Passion Principles

Pathways To Purpose, Power, & Profit!

Praise for The Passion Principles

"Discovering the passions in your life, will lead you to understanding your purpose in life. I thoroughly enjoyed reading it, and have begun to work on areas of my life that need my attention."

Sheila Tolbert
Training Manager
Amoco Corporation

" I found The Passion Principles to be both educational and enjoyable. Zelda's down-to-earth perspective will no doubt be helpful to anyone to improve their life skills."

D. Van Tran,
Acting Dean
Continuing Education
Truman College - Chicago

"A collection of compelling stories illustrating life's lessons are learned on the journey when you make a conscious decision to live your purpose passionately!"

O'Merrial Butchee'
President, Chicago Chapter
National African American Speakers Association

"This Book is truly a gift…it offers us a way to live our lives with the joy and passion we need to achieve the magnificent life that we deserve. However, the real gift is that of Zelda herself…it is her willingness to share utterly of herself, which makes it worth reading, because it gives us the opportunity to experience Zelda's beautiful and shining essence. Read this book *only* if you are ready to embrace the exquisiteness of life.

-Caroline Gatten, LCSW
Speaker/Trainer/Author
Founder, Chicagoland Association for Self-Esteem

The Passion Principles,
Pathways To Purpose, Power, & Profit!

Zelda Robinson

Printed in the United States of America.

Cover Design by Ilaiyah Dorsey

Editing by Carol Hibler

ISBN 1-890896-50-0

Library of Congress Catalog Card Number: 99-90098

Published by:

PASSION PUBLISHING

a subsidiary of Zelda Robinson Communications
Speaking/Trainer Consulting/Seminars/Workshops
P.O. BOX 118305
Chicago, Illinois 60611

Order Information

To order more copies of this book or to receive a complete catalog of other products by ZRC:
Zelda Robinson Communications contact:

PASSION PUBLISHING

Bus. (312) 642-4449 Fax (312) 642-4429

email: Zelda@zeldaspeaks.com
website: http://www.zeldaspeaks.com

Acknowledgments

-To The *Creator*, who has pushed me since 1991, to send this message through me, despite my trying to hold it back.

-*Vivian Foster*, my big sister who always knew that I had greatness within me, even before Les Brown coined the phrase.

-*Les Brown*, The Motivator, my mentor, who inspired me to move beyond the comfort of the microphone in the radio studio, and into the speaking arena of life.

-*Dr. Johnnie Coleman,* my spiritual mentor, for allowing Spirit to use you, and for being a ray of light in my life. Thank you!

-*John H. Johnson*, for giving me my first job in radio as Radio Personality, and having a station that would allow me to utilize my radio skills, which evolved into the professional speaking arena.

-*P.J. Willis*, first Program Director that hired me, that didn't require an audition on the *casting couch*.

-*Inez Clay,* my old school sisterfriend, who's always been there for me.

-*Debra Wright,* publisher of The Wright Stuff, who supported me from day one before I even began writing the book.

-*Linda Hicks-Profit*, author of "Celebrations", and my Leo sisterfriend, who always reminds me to be more loving to myself.

-*Linda Shepard*, my dearest Sisterfriend and workout partner, who reminds me that I don't have to hide from myself anymore.

-*Sharon Bradley,* my niece who is the daughter I always wanted and who reminds me of the possibilities.

-*Sheila Glasnov*, my Jewish Soul Sister, for your support!

-*Eddie,* Thanks for the lessons, especially the ones I didn't want to learn. Look in the mirror!

-*Francine Barron*, the greatest creative mind and marketing consultant on planet earth.

-*Grethia Hightower,* counselor and sisterfriend who always encourages me to do more.

-*Vanessa,* sisterfriend and research buddy, thanks for the insight.
-*Doc*, Thanks for being my friend, when I needed someone to talk to.
-*Cindy DuBois,* my massage therapist whose healing hands and inspirational conversation keeps me coming back for more.
-*Mama Kelly,* who adopted me as her own daughter, who always makes me feel welcomed and lets me take a plate home.
-*Pee Wee Nixon,* for always making me feel like a part of the family.
-*Julie*, for letting me know when supplies were on sale, so I could stock up.
-*Barbara Tousaint*, for always having her heart and refrigerator door open.
-*Chub, I* can always count on you for a good, l-o-n-g laugh, when I need one.
-*Mechelle Williams*, turntable Sister who helped me get my first job in radio.
-*Toni Turner*, author of *Love Gone Wrong and Wisdom for the Soul*, who rekindled the idea to write this book.
-*LaKeisha Tanksley*, author of *There is an Oasis*, who is always ready to assist me with publishing tips, and words of inspiration.
-*Sporty King & Associates*, author of *Spoetry* ™, his words of encouragement and sharing his knowledge of the publishing industry.
-*Tami Brent*, T&D Trainer Director, Commonwealth Edison, my first Fortune 500 Client. A real down to earth sisterfriend.
Dr. Charles Pitchford, of the United Kingdom, for offering me my first *international* speaking engagement.
-*A.G. Muteshi*-Chairman, Institute of Personnel Management, Nairobi, Kenya, East Africa, my second *international* client, for the wonderful experience of a lifetime.
-*Pacifica,* Mr. Muteshi's Executive Secretary, who made my presentation and visit most enjoyable.
Don Crutchfield, for your friendship and advice on binding.
-*Chuck Parham,* for the experience of touring 50 states.

-*Hope Daniels*, *Columbia College Radio Instructor*, who pushed me the extra mile, inspiring me to work more on developing my broadcast technique.
Jay Allan, Asst. PD- WGCI 107.5, for having faith in me during the WJPC/106 JAMZ transition.
-*Loren Devaroe*, my sweetest Sisterfriend, right hand, and Producer.
-*Marsha Noble*, my left hand, ex producer, radio personality, playwright, and good friend.
*Gene Phillips,(*The Original *Airman)* who helped me hone my production skills.
-*Mary M. Berger, of The Speak Standard Too Institute*, for making me feel comfortable with my southern dialect.
-*Bam*, Barbara A. McDowell, my producer/friend, who is always willing to help.
Denise Jordan Walker, my spiritual sister and friend, for welcoming me to the world of radio.
*LaDonna Tittle, (*Your Tittle in the Middle*)*whom I listened to while in college, for your sisterly advice on the entertainment industry.
Effie Rolfe, my sister of the arts, for your love and support.
-*Co-workers and staff of V103/106 JAMZ*, and *WGCI*, for your love and support.
-*Zig Ziglar*, who allowed me the opportunity to experience wisdom from a professional point of view that included insights on spirituality and longevity in the speaking industry.
-*My family*, both biological and extended, who love me, just the way I am.
-All of the success story participants who shared their lives with my readers.

Dedication

I'll never forget the first day I walked into the studio of WGCI - FM, and saw this beautiful woman, with hair flowing in every direction, sitting in the studio doing her thing. I was in total awe. It was a new beginning for me, interning as a News Assistant at the number one station in Chicago, and getting a chance to see my favorite performer, Chaka Kahn. I ran back to the news room so excited, telling my then News Director, Perry Williams that I had seen Chaka Kahn. He simply laughed and informed me that it wasn't Chaka Kahn, it was mid-day host, Shannon Dell. Disappointed, but still excited, I went back in the studio, this time, getting a good look. Sure enough, there was Shannon, doing what she did best. I introduced myself, and the conversation that followed, was one I will always cherish. I wish I had been wise enough at the time to read between the lines, but I wasn't.

Anyone who knows anything about the history of women, know that even in western society, advanced as it is, women are still considered second class citizens. In this business, women are still treated as sidekicks to a male host. As Radio Personality A.J. Parker refers to it as an automatic giggle box. Shannon was no giggle box, and her ratings proved it. Although she fought for a higher salary and better working conditions, she lost the battle, but in doing so, she paved the way for other women to work in the industry.

As a role model, her talent was an inspiration to countless of young women studying radio. As a champion of women's rights, women can still envision themselves making a difference, and fighting for what they believe in. Like many before her, including Yvonne Daniel's, formerly of WNUA, Shannon paved the way for myself and many others that will follow.

Let the truth be told that in the case of Karen Grace Jones, was one who fought, and lost the battle, but it was not in vain. Shannon fought for what was right. But what's fair, does not always win. In the quest for pursuing our passion in life, let us be reminded, not to let our passion consume us. Throughout our lives, new opportunities and challenges will appear. Some of them acceptable, others not. It is when life presents us challenges that we have absolutely no control over, we must learn to let go. As ancient scripture says, Be Still, and know. Be still and know that the Universe has something else, bigger and better in store for us. When we let go of stuff, then we can move on, ready to accept that which has been prepared for us. Shannon Dell has moved on, to a bigger and better place. We miss you, our mid-day diva, thank you for your contribution, and will continue to "*Love you like a sister.*" Rest in peace, Shannon Dell.

A Special Note of Thanks

To Ms. Mary M. Berger
THE SPEAK STANDARD TOO INSTITUTE

I had the pleasure of meeting this young woman, who was my speech coach class while studying radio at Columbia College in Chicago. This petite woman packs a powerful punch in the form of the truth in which she so lovingly shares with her students. This remarkable woman, so vibrant, so full of the blessing that was bestowed upon her, is truly an earth angel.

Not only did she make me feel comfortable with the southern drawl I had adopted from living a few years in the South, she made me realize that the heritage from which I came was worthy despite the general consensus in Corporate America. Her ability to put students at ease, whether they had a Southern drawl, New Yorker accent or Midwestern flavor, was a real blessing in disguise. It reassured me that there was still a chance for me in radio, despite the nay-sayers.

She provided us all with a sense of direction, where the path often ends just because of the dialect in which you speak. Those words will forever linger in my memory. "Your dialect is simply different, not deficient." That thought has carried me for the few short years I have been in radio, and in the speaking industry. For that Ms. Berger, I am eternally grateful..

SPEAK STANDARD TOO INSTITUTE
2222 North Orchard Street
Chicago, Ill. 60614
1-800-528-5244
email: dialect2@aol.com

Table of Contents

Foreword by God

01/06/99 3:56 AM

I told her in 1989, but she didn't hear me. I told her again in 1990, but by that time, she was so caught up in doing so many other things, she really didn't pay much attention to me. As she grew older and somewhat wiser, I kept thinking to myself, maybe one day soon she will hear me.

Then in 1991, the bug hit. She began journaling. She wasn't writing what I had asked her, but at least it was a beginning. When she went back to college to study broadcasting after an eight year absence, she really put me on the back burner. After graduation in 1993, she was too busy working at two radio stations to even think about me then.

The plans I had for her. But she just couldn't hear me. She listened when she needed an answer. She would even take time to go within and quite herself consistently. Morning mediation. Journaling. Even mediation. She was getting good at it. She even shared her meditation techniques with friends and co-workers. She was really beginning to make a difference, or so she thought. But she still didn't hear me.

Then all of a sudden as a if a bolt of lightening slapped her, she stopped. She listened. She heard. She obeyed. It was at a social gathering where she was making small talk with friends and colleagues in the radio industry. A young lady whom she did not know, began talking about what kind of books they liked. Then the conversation turned around to talking about men.

Well wouldn't you know it? The lady that she was talking to, just happened to have written a book on both subjects. Without hesitancy, and with the prestige as if she was whipping out an American Express Card, Tony Turner, author of Love Gone Wrong, handed Zelda a copy of her book.

She browsed through it and was immediately inspired. She shared with Tony how she had started writing some years ago, and never finished. She wanted to write a book, but didn't know what exactly what. Tony, an international airline steward, offered her words of encouragement and Zelda began the process of taking her years of journaling putting it into book form.

As the years pass, Zelda kept in contact with Tony, calling her sometimes asking questions about the publishing business. Well, by now Zelda is an accomplished international Professional/Speaker/Training Consultant/Radio/TV Personality, and she has a little experience to share with her listening audience.

Zelda gave herself the best KWANZA present she's ever given herself. 1997 comes to a close with a completed manuscript. It took all of 1998 to complete the editing, because Zelda was afraid to move forward.

She completed the book, but was still carrying baggage from her childhood years, wondering what would people say about her writing ability. She was afraid that she would offend some people. She was afraid that someone might challenge her on something she said in the book.

Now it's 1999. The book was due to be released December 1, 1998. The manuscript is still sitting on her desk. She can't locate (Zelda, can't locate? Impossible!) the person that she wants to write the forward for the book. So it sits on her desk. Then late one evening as she was watching Iyanla Vanzant on Oprah, she heard Iyanla say, "There is nothing in this world that a child of God can't do, who has his hand, in the hand, of God." With that thought in mind, Zelda turned on her laptop, and asked me to write the foreword. She finally heard, my still, small voice.

This my friends, is what you have been waiting for. I highly recommend that you read this book. Why? Because just as I speak to her, I speak to you in the same small voice. She listened. Will you?

Yours Truly,
Father, Mother God.
I AM that I AM.
And so it is.

Introduction

Finding one's purpose in life is no easy task. Some people know sooner than others. It's taken me 38 years to discover, that Speaking/Training Consulting, Workshops is what lights up my life! I've always known that my voice was my gift from the Universe, I just had not quite figured out how to channel it. Working as a Receptionist, Switchboard Operator, Secretary, Voice-over artist, Clerk, Telemarketer, Girl-Friday, Crisis Counselor and Reading Interpreter were all fine for the time being, but that was not the reason for my being here on this planet. There was more to life than sounding pleasant while talking on the telephone.

A great portion of my life has been spent on the telephone. I have the phone bills to prove it. I was sitting in the studio at the radio station (of what was then known as WJPC, which is now V103/106 JAMZ, WEJM) at the microphone, waiting for the midnight shift to end, and the morning crew to come in. I was filling in for Traci Dion, waiting for Chicago's own "Heavy Duty Cutey", as he was affectionately referred to.
As much as I loved playing the "dusties" for the folks working the night shift, and the "regulars" who kept calling me saying, "I Can't Go To Sleep 'Cause You Jammin" Too Strong", I knew that there was something missing. There was something else I was supposed to be doing, I just didn't know what. So I'd take another caller with a request, and play another "Strong Song". (The station's identification hook, as in V103's Best Variety of Hits and Dusties, or WNUA's Smooth Jazz)

My passion for radio was still there, but the uncertainty of job security always lingered in the back of my mind. I knew from day one, before I was even hired for the position of on-air talent

(Radio Personality), that longevity was not in the cards for anyone, especially women. Long gone are the days of celebrating 50 years in the industry, as a Radio Personality. Herb Kent is the only one who had that kind of success in our genre of music.

Much to my surprise, I survived the first two changes in management, which caused even more confusion about what else I should be doing with my life. Should I continue to pursue this career, and take it to another level, is the question I would ask myself? Having always enjoyed listening, and studying the messages from motivational tapes, I decided that this was something else I could do, besides voice-overs. I produced the first one for myself, and a friend from New York heard it and ask for one, and this is where the journey began.

Years of listening to the best in motivation, Zig Ziglar, Og Mandingo, Tony Robins, Florence Scovel Shinn, Les Brown, Rev. Johnny Coleman, Rev. Jeremiah Wright, Brian Tracey, George Fraser, Steven Covey, Dr. Dennis Waitley, W. Clement Stone, Dr. Norman Vincent Peale, Dr. Bernie Siegel, Ernest Holmes, and recently, Inyanla Vanzant, and countless others, have finally paid off. Once I found out that Les Brown was coming to Chicago to teach his "Speaking For A Living Seminar", I knew that this was my chance to make a difference in my life.

As Murphy's Law would have it, circumstances prevented me from attending that workshop. I vowed to myself, that next year I would attend, No Matter What Happened! I kept that promise to myself. To this day, that was the best career choice I've made since graduation from Columbia College with a degree in Broadcast Communications. It only took me eight years to graduate from a four year institution, but I did it I realize that college is not an option for everyone, but reading is for the benefit of everyone. If there is something that I can say that will make a difference in the lives of those who read this, then I will have completed my purpose, through this book. All the years of reading, listening to motivational cassettes, attending seminars and workshops have led me to this point in life.

What I share with you through these pages, is only a small sample of what Spirit channels through me. I cannot take full responsibility for the messages that reach you, because I am still a student of the principles (Purpose, Acceptance, Surrender, Setting Realistic Goals, Inventory, Obstacles, Now) in which I teach. I a still learning myself. May the words of these pages, reach you inspire you and point you in the direction of fulfilling your purpose in this life. This my friend, is the purpose of The Passion Principles. Enjoy!

Chapter 1

Purpose

A job pays the rent
training for a vocation, provides you with a career
your passion is the journey,
in which your purpose unfolds

-Linda Shepard
Program Manager, Career Links
Women Employed

Pay attention to the breath. It is the essence of all living things. At that point in life when we become attuned to our breathing, our awareness begins to change. We become more receptive to what the Universe is saying to us. We begin to live life fully, hopefully, from a sense of urgency, and expectancy.

Not necessarily needing to know the who, what, when, where, and how. We, always, always need to be concerned with the ***why***. *Why are we here?* Without a doubt, to discover and embrace our purpose in life, and to act from that state of ecstasy, or passion. Full time, not some time, or part time, but all of the time. That's the sole purpose of The Passion Principles, to assist you on your journey of living life to the fullest.

The Passion Principles, (*Purpose, Acceptance, Surrender, Setting Priorities, Inventory, Obstacles, Now!*) are essential elements in living life according to the divine plan. Principles are similar to Universal laws. Universal laws are consistent.

They never change. Only people change. The sun coming up the next day, and the moon coming out at night, is the Universal Law in full force. It never changes. Why? The Universe has a set rotation, governed by God, that never fails. That's why it's important to never put your faith in man, but in a higher power, that will never change.

Your breath is a prime example of Universal Law at work. You will always be able to breath as long as you don't obstruct the passage in which air has to flow. As long as you are breathing, you have the opportunity to experience life, as you never have before. The moment you stop breathing, another force has to step in and take over for you. (Such as a breathing apparatus, oxygen, etc.) You can't live without breath, so you may as well master it.

Stop for a moment and notice your breathing pattern. Do you take long deep breaths? Do you breathe through your mouth or nose? Do you feel your chest rise as you inhale? Do you feel your chest deflate as you exhale, or are you still waiting to exhale? In other words, is your breathing so shallow, that you barely notice that you are breathing?

Our breathing represents our capacity to take in life. Full breaths allow the fullness of the Universe to operate within us. Shallow breathing keeps us in our comfort zones, where we stay stuck. Check on your breathing from time to time, especially when you're frustrated or tense. Notice the pattern. Start taking long, deep breaths through your nostrils the next time you're in a tense situation, and notice the difference in the shift of how you handle that situation.

Shallow breathing is like working a part-time job. You can't work part-time and expect to get full time benefits. It doesn't work that way. Plain and simple. If you want the benefits of full time work, then you must apply yourself accordingly. Life is just like breathing. Long, deep breaths, breathe in the fullness of life. Short breaths, circumvent life. I would strongly suggest to anyone who is serious about living, and breathing fully, to take yoga instruction class, or rent a video on the subject.

Every since I was a little girl, I had been curious about yoga, because I saw this very skinny lady on television practicing it, every day. I also wanted to be skinny, and be able to wrap my legs around the back of my neck. Well, I never slimmed down to anywhere near as skinny as the lady on television is, nor can I wrap my legs behind my head. But what has happened is that I am now able to bend over and touch my toes, bend my body backwards and forwards without grunting, and without being in pain.

So many of my friends and colleagues in their forties, can't even bend over and touch their toes, without grunting like stuck pigs. That may not seem like much, unless you try to do it, and you can't. Yoga strengthens the muscles of the mind, as well as the body. I urge you to try a yoga class and notice the difference in your breathing, and in your life.

That one class has made a considerable difference in the quality of my life. I am not always at peace with every situation in my life, but I am aware of the changes that my body is experiencing in a stressful period. Awareness of stress, and how to handle it, can easily diffuse a harmful damaging environment. I still practice my breathing techniques, though I don't always practice the yoga stretching exercises on a daily basis.

What I really like about the breathing techniques, is that you can practice them anywhere, anytime. I really had to practice them while trying to balance going to school full time, and working full time, at the Chicago Board of Trade. It was such a fun job, but it was too hectic, and it had begun to get the best of me.

Sitting at my desk at 6:45 am, on the 14th floor of the Chicago Board of Trade Building, waiting to open up the switchboard to answer thousands of calls that would flood the brokers desk, I asked myself, *Why am I doing this*? Mechanically, a voice answered, because you've got rent to pay, followed up with refrain: besides, you love what you do. As the muzak-like response sank in, tightening the chains of comfort and ease, I asked myself another question. Well, couldn't you find another job that doesn't start at seven in the morning? A taunting answer appeared, as quickly as the question did saying, sure you could, but you'd probably be bored to death even more than you are now. Not to mention the fact that you'd have to go to the same office every single day and deal with the same people, doing the same things, telling the same lies, playing the same games. This was not a career move, just part of the journey. It's a life long journey, to answering the question that no one has the answer to, except you.

The answer to all my problems has usually been to eat something sweet, and the problem, would appear to have like a magic act, and simply disappear, for the moment anyway. I made lots of food disappear on a regular basis too. Pretty good for a non magician. The one thing I have *obsessed* over most, is food, or a lack of it. It comes from my childhood years, when my mom (Katie) died, and I was sent to Mississippi to live with an aunt. My aunt Edna, had two great big, old, "Mean Joe Green", romp'em, stomp'em, eat up everything in sight" sons, who didn't care one way or the other if anyone else got anything to eat. Since my aunt did the cooking, naturally she would fix her plate first, and let them go for it. My cousins did not act out of animosity, they were just used to eating until their hearts content. Still, that meant that I was often left with little to eat.

That was then. This is now. (Isn't it strange how we allow our past to run our present lives?) O.K. My days are too frequently consumed with the same nagging thoughts of what I will eat at any given time, and it doesn't have to be that way. I have two of the greatest cooks in the world, (my sister Vivian and cousin Barbara) who always have food in their refrigerator, and I am always welcome, with my Tupperware. I know fresh food is better, but I am still working on that too. When you know better, you do better, right? Wrong. When you know better, you're *supposed* to do better. Sometimes I do what's best for my health, sometimes I don't. Since I don't cook as often as I should, and won't take the time to grocery shop on a regular basis, I usually wind up eating junk foods.

How does that relate to my personal passion? Every since I was old enough to know what the word passion meant, I longed for physical passion, for someone to be as passionate about me, as I would be about them. After so many years of drifting in and out of relationships, it finally dawned on me one day, that the kind of passion I was seeking, could never come from anything outside of myself, or from someone else. It had to come from within.

I am the only person in the world who can fulfill my own passion. It is a passion for *life*, not *lust*, that I am seeking. The kind of passion that would have you in love with the mere fact you were alive and breathing, with an opportunity to live the quality of life you desire and to make a difference in this world. To wake up every morning, and do something different than you did yesterday, not to be bogged down by routine and live life from a hum drum existence. I know how that feels. Been there, done that, burned that T-shirt. Through the process of discovering who I am, I now know that my true passion, is allowing spirit to speak through me, in my career as a speaker and training consultant on personal and professional development. That's my full time passion. That is what drives me from day to day. Now my part time passion, that's another story.

Part Time Passion

While studying photojournalism at Columbia College in Chicago, I was on my first assignment, covering a fire. The remains of the fire were too much for me to handle. I could not, in good conscious, impose on a grieving mother, who had just lost her children in a fire, by sticking a camera lens in her face, and asking her how she felt. It was at that moment, that I knew that this was not going to be my career choice. As much as I loved photography, (I had been freelancing for five years, I could not go on doing this type of work.)

Unsatisfied with my choice of studies, I took my time while leafing through the fall course catalog to determine what my next major would be for the coming semester. After taking one television class, I dropped out and decided that maybe radio would be a better choice. Besides, I always knew that my voice is my talent, I just had not found out how to channel it properly. Radio felt like the right thing to do. So I hitched up my wagon, and got on the road, again, to continue my journey.

My first day in my Introduction to Radio class, I knew I had found my niche. I lived for Tuesday mornings to turn in my assignments. I was 36 years old, and finally finding something, outside of eating, that made me stay up until the wee hours of the morning, and it wasn't late night bingeing. It was a major breakthrough for me, though I didn't realize it then. I wasn't really living, just going through a routine like a lot of other folks.

Too many people are half living their lives. They're half happy, half healthy, and some have no hope at all. Do you know anyone like this? Look around, you'll see them everywhere. Not only on the corners, hanging out doing nothing, but in the office and boardrooms of Corporate America too. They are members of our communities, our spouses, and yes, our families too. We see them, and sometimes identify them by their speech pattern. They often speak in a low voice, sometimes in an over-bearing voice and sometimes they don't even speak at all.

We distinguish them by the pattern of their walk. They walk sometimes with shoulders slumped over, heads down, and just to throw us off, they even walk with their heads held high, with a great big reassuring smile of confidence on their cheery faces. Clearly we are familiar with these people because, of course, they are mirrors of ourselves. We are all reflections of one another. We could not see something in someone else, if we did not see it in ourselves first. Sounds startling? The truth often is. It's sometime painful, and may cause us to immediately go into denial. It may not be evident right now, but at some point in time it's a reality.

We sometimes live our life as if it was a part time job. We want the benefits that a full time job offers, but we don't want to give a full day's work. We want to experience the joys of life, but we we're not always willing to do the work necessary to take us there. In essence, we want to receive, but we don't want to give. Universal Law doesn't work that way. You only get in life, what you are willing to work for.

Not everyone's passion stops at the end of the workday. My dearest friend, mentor, and spiritual advisor, who makes me look at myself, when I really don't want to, is a lady I admire most. Her passion goes way beyond the call of duty. She has taken a local community program, stirred it up with all the love, and care she could find, and it has grown phenomenally within the last five years, like you wouldn't believe.

Linda Shepard
Activist, Community Leader
Linda Shepard & Associates

If you ever get within earshot of this woman, you're automatically enlisted. As Program Director of Women Employed's Career Links, a career based group mentor program for teenage girls, Linda's passion is self evident. She walks the talk. Her mission is to offer these teens the opportunity to explore the possibilities of not only careers they may have never even heard of, but more importantly, discover something good in themselves. These young girls are inner city youth, many who haven't been exposed to very little outside of their immediate communities. Linda trains adult women to help teen girls realize their potential.

Linda brings with her, the experience of having been a married teen mother who was severely abused by an alcoholic husband. She shares her life as an extension of the possibilities of what can happen when given exposure to different opportunities.

Linda left a six figure salary, a prominent position on California's Regional Transit Authority Board, her own consulting business, and a political career with the administration of both President Jimmy Carter, and then Speaker, Willie Brown, Jr.'. She came to Chicago to care for her terminally ill father. (see Chicago Tribune article in WomanNews, December 1996)

Linda had extraordinary success in the business and political arena, but was forced with making a pivotal decision. After her fathers death, she had to decide if she would go back to her previous work in California, making enormous amounts of money, or would she stay in Chicago and seek a new direction outside of politics. She joined a church and got involved in volunteer activities at Women Employed. Money was not an immediate issue, because she had enough to live comfortably for a few years, until she decided what she wanted to do. She decided to stay, accepting a position at Women Employed, as Program Director of the Mentoring Program for teen girls.

It didn't matter that the salary offered was less than half of her previous salary, she had finally found her calling, her passion in life. This was not work! This was her chance to do all the things she loved doing! This was her chance to really make a difference in the lives of people she cared about the most, our youth, especially, teen girls.

She's taken Career Links to a variety of communities in the city of Chicago and the nation. As Program Director she has successfully made the program available through various organizations throughout the city, including the mentoring component which is offered at Abraham Lincoln Center, Greer Residential Center, St. Josephinums High School, the Cook County Department of Corrections Juvenile Detention Center, Christ Universal Temple, Chicago Park District, and the Chicago Board of Education. I am honored to be a mentor at several of the sites.

Linda's greatest challenge is learning what makes it okay for Linda to take care of everyone except Linda. Her assessment is that "it comes from a feeling of not feeling worthy. When you grow up in an environment that is not loving and nurturing, you carry those feelings into your adult life, and they manifest in different ways. We carry those feelings of unworthiness into our careers, our families, and our lives. That's one of the reasons that this mentoring program is so important, to let the young girls know that they have a support system available to them. Someone is there to listen, if nothing else."

Her best advise to anyone, is to be careful of how you treat people. Linda says, "There's three things you can never take back. That's a day gone, a deed done, and a word spoken.

Always check with your higher power, before you say or do something, and you will never go wrong."

Linda remembers a situation where the conversation was not particularly pleasant, and she had to think to herself for a moment. Before she spoke, she ask herself, "What would God do? Before I open my mouth, let the God in me, connect with the God in them, no matter who they are. People sometimes say things they really don't mean. You may be the only bible, they ever read."

Linda is an example of someone living on purpose, with passion. She chose to work at something she simply loves doing, which is really a joy. She could have gone back to another job with a higher salary making a ton more money, with fabulous fringe benefits, but she chose a line of work that brings her joy. As Linda says, her joy is in her work, and her passion for what she does, has allowed her to find her purpose, as she continues the journey. After all, your work should be play, and the pay is just the bonus.

Linda is an example of Spirit living a power life filled with purpose and passion! This amazing woman's life epitomizes the phrase *when life gives you lemons - make lemonade*! Linda was married, with 4 children, battered by her addicted husband, permanently disabled and separated by age 20. She was well on her way to becoming another social service statistic.

Instead, she has several college degrees, an impressive career which includes being elected to public office for 8 years, and owning a legislative consulting business for 10 year with some of California's most powerful elite as clients. Her business and personal travels have taken her high into the mountains of Ecuador, to Europe, Africa and 45 of 50 US states. She has enjoyed holiday's on some the worlds most fashionable white sand filled beach resorts. Her passion and drive have taken her a long way from the rat infested tenements where she grew up in St. Louis. She enjoyed a lucrative business with a 6 figure salary until a family emergency made it necessary for her to relocate to Chicago indefinitely to care for her dying parent.

Linda decided not to return to the fast paced non stop political lifestyle, but remain in Chicago and start a new life doing the work that called to her Spirit! Working with a non-for-profit organization. Linda developed Chicago's most successful mentor program for teen girls. A citywide career based group mentor program with professional women working with inner city teen girls, many of the girls are teen mothers with 1 or more children. With a volunteer pool of over 500 women the program provides service to 11 organizations and reaching 1000 - 1500 teen girls annually. She is a firm believer in "none of us is successful without help - pass it on".

Linda recently decided to leave the non-for-profit community and embark on a new career endeavor. As a Management Consultant, She will provide program development and organizational skills to business, government, social and community service organizations. Throughout her career Linda has always remained faithful to her church. She believes that we all have more gifts than we could possibly use in one life time. The most powerful messages adults send our young, is seen, not heard. We must be passionate, successful spirits and not do successful things! Her formula for success: Prayer + meditation + action = passion!

Chapter 2

Acceptance

"While I know myself as a creation of God, I am also obligated to realize and remember everyone else and everything else are also God's creation."

-Dr. Maya Angelou

One of the most challenging things on this earth to do, is simply be yourself. Why? Because we are always comparing ourselves to something or someone else. Why is that? Because society influences our every waking moment, whether we realize it or not.

From the moment we rise in the morning, until we go to bed at night.
from the moment the alarm clock wakes us up,
what kind of soap we shower with,
what we drink or don't drink,
what we eat, with or without raisins,
the type of house we live in, the neighborhood,
the clothes we wear (this is a global fashion conspiracy)
the type of car we drive,
what kind of job we have,
where we work,
where the best vacation spot is,
what's hot, what's not,
what to read,

- who to date,
- who to marry,
- who not to associate with,
- who to network with,
- where the best deals are made,
- on the greens,
- over lunch,
- in the office,
- chambers,
- what we read,
- what we listen to,

  and last but not least,
- what we see. (with the physical eye)

Most of my childhood, and adult life, I have always compared myself to others, and naturally, I have never been satisfied. As a kid, I was always too tall for my age, too thin, nose too big, glasses too thick, hair too short and nappy, knock-kneed and pigeon toed. Did I forget to mention they called me Dumbo? How could I forget that nickname? With ears the size of half of a small ear of corn, I was damaged for life. I wore scarves around my ears all day, every single day, until I was an adult. I had been conditioned since birth, that in order to be accepted in this world, that I had to look a certain way, or I would not fit in. This was the conditioning of a society that does not respect individuality, especially if that individual comes from a lower socio-economic community.

Programming at it's best. Conditioning, plain and simple. Just like it is on television and on the radio. What we pay money for, earned by the sweat of our brow, we may have purchased because of an advertisement we saw on television, or heard on the radio. Now, I'm not saying that's a bad thing, because advertising is sometimes effective. It's that kind of consuming, that concerns me. As consumers, we need to be more selective in our choices. Don't buy something just because it's the *in* thing to buy.

Whether we believe it or not, we are all conditioned, one way or another. For those who are unfamiliar with the inner workings of the radio industry, there is a special department that schedules or programs every single record we hear. The days are over where radio personalities play what they want to hear. Except in smaller markets, practically everything that we watch on video, in the theater, at the opera, and television, is programmed. TV is the most programmed event of the hour.

If you don't this is true, check your local television or cable guide. Notice the hourly programs? Notice the commercials? What do they say to us? We're not good enough as we are, we need certain things in our lives to make us more attractive, lovable, etc. The craze of the personal home computer is a prime example of media hype of a product. By the time you purchase your first computer from the store, it is already obsolete. There is another computer, sitting in a warehouse, waiting to be shipped to the stores.

After a few months on the market, then the latest PC will once again be obsolete. I remember when I bought my first 386 home computer. By the time I became familiar with it, (after it sat on my desk for six months before I used it. I was still using secretarial services to type my letters and proposals) technology had moved on. The 486 was out, and by the time I was ready to update, the Pentium was the latest thing to have.

Now it's Pentium II. At the rate of constant upgrades, how will you ever keep up? So you have to know where to draw the line.

We have to know what's acceptable in our lives. What we can live with, and what we can live without. I accept the fact, that I will probably won't always have the latest technology in PC's. My Pentium meets my needs. I can live with that. As I become more aware of the conditioning, the programming that already exists in my life, I have to ask myself the question, "Is this something I need, or something I want? If it's not a need, like basic survival need: food, clothing, shelter, etc., everything else is a desire. A programmed desire, no less.

PROGRAMS
PROGRAMMED
FOR PROGRAMMING
THE PROGRAMMER

Just for you and I. The few, the proud, the programmed.

Case scenario:

A young girl grows up in a foreign country, brought here by her ancestors, to live among the new foreigners. None of the people that she come in contact with outside of her family environment, look, speak, or act like anyone she knows. While growing up, she goes to the local school, where she has to contend with being called out of her name because she doesn't have pretty clothing, long curly flowing hair, or candy money, let alone lunch money. She's lucky to be in school at all. *The young girl is afforded conditional acceptance based upon how she fits with the program.*

This **PROGRAM** was already in high gear upon her arrival, and the fact that she was allowed to maybe fit in, was further **PROGRAMMING**. As she grew older and saw less and less of images in the media that depicted what she saw in the mirror on a daily basis, she began to dislike herself even more, because she did not fit the mole, the model, or the **PROGRAM**. She carried these images with her well into her adult years. She had a family, a little girl, like she once was herself, and now the cycle continues.

The **PROGRAMMED,** gets to be the **PROGRAMMER**. She will **PROGRAM** her children, who in turn will **PROGRAM** their children. The saga of **PROGRAMMING** continues. The cycle doesn't stop until someone who is not as **PROGRAMABLE,** stops, and maybe scrambles the channels enough so that they can begin to think on their own, without the assistance of a **PROGRAMMER**. One way to do that is to limit yourself from artificial stimuli.

Everything you usually listen to or watch on television is fictitious and really does more damage than it does good. Try doing just the opposite. If you've always watched the evening news, turn off the television and read a chapter from a book. If you stop to think about it for a moment, what did you really miss? If it's something you really needed to know, someone will call you and tell you about it. Or you're likely to hear about it in a conversation the next day anyway. If what you heard, did not help you in any way enhance your life, you were better off without it. The probability of your hearing something on the evening news that will enhance the quality of your life is slightly less than your chance of wining the lottery, without a winning ticket.

Turning off the television was a big step for me. I figured out a way to watch my programs and read self help books at the same time. With the help of modern technology, I would record my favorite shows on the VCR, and save them until it was my allotted television time. Needless to say, the programs I taped, I never had time to see all of them. When I did turn them on to watch, they usually watched me instead. So now, I had to break the habit of falling asleep with the television on.

Wasted time **PROGRAMMING** them into the VCR, and wasted money on unnecessary video tapes that sat and collected dust. Now this was totally unacceptable behavior. Wasting time and money. Certain things we accept without question, some things we will not accept under any circumstances. Besides, I was running out of places to put the video tapes. Though we accept a good deal of the garbage that is dumped on us in our lives, the hardest thing to accept is of course, ourselves.

UNACCEPTABLE ACCEPTANCE

It's taken quite a long time to accept myself, just as I am. Big hips, big ears, and a big smile to match. I'm not so much concerned about the size of the body parts anymore. It's the physical condition of my body, the energy and the stamina that I have, that's more important. The fact that I can walk or run up eight flights of stairs (thanks to my personal trainer) and continue working out for another 30 minutes or an hour, without passing out, means more to me than any size.

Many of my friends and colleagues who are half my size, don't have the stamina I have. They wonder where I get it from.

It comes from within. We all have it, we just haven't taken the time to develop it. OK, if it means getting up at up five am, going into the gym, getting on the bike or treadmill by seven, then that's what you have to do.

Never did I ever imagine that I would get out of the warmth and comfort of my bed to go to anyone's gym, training facility or any other place that early in the morning to do anything, except maybe pick up a check. It had better be a big one. When you get to the point in your life, where you turn over to roll out of the bed in the morning to get up, and you notice that some parts of your body have yet to catch up with the rest of your body, you need to do something different. All body parts should move together, in tandem. That's how life works. Why should our bodies be any different?

If you're healthy, you don't walk to the store on one leg, and stop at every other step to drag the other leg wagging behind you. The steps you take, should be in synchronized together. When the mind and body attuned, we develop a new consciousness that just does not allow us to operate out of the old thinking patterns that have held us hostage for so long.

It is in this state of consciousness of having a situation in our lives that we can no longer accept, that we have to do something different. As my favorite instructor, Rev. Evelyn Boyd of Christ Universal Temple, who says, "You can't keep putting new ideas in an old container. It's like putting new wine, in old wineskins. You gotta clear out the old before you can add the new stuff." That's Universal Law. Always has been. Always will be.

That's why I have always lost the weight, but have always gained it back. I had the physical part, the working out, down to a science. Aerobics five days a week , and weight training three days, with a personal trainer. An exercise regimen was vital to the success of my weight loss program, but what was even more vital, was the process of getting in touch with whatever it was that was causing me to eat out of stress, in the first place.

It had become such a habit, that the moment anything bothered me, I would grab something, anything, to put in my mouth, to stuff down the feelings that I was having, because I didn't want to feel what I was feeling. I didn't want to feel the pain. Who does? This kind of behavior went on for so very, very long, forty one years to be exact, but it had gotten to the point where it made me angry. It made me not feel good about myself. I had carried this feeling for so long, that it became acceptable That is unacceptable acceptance. It was time to move on. Besides, it's my smile that everyone seems to enjoy anyway. It's my smile that my family, friends, and colleagues and participants seem to care about most. I thank all of you who saw past my faults, and recognized my needs.

I've lived most of my adult life, like most adults, from the outside in, instead of the other way around. I've worked jobs I hated just because someone convinced me I would be good at it. Sound familiar? I've been involved in relationships that would not have worked regardless of the circumstances, but because I didn't take the time (or know how) to examine the pros and cons of things, I weathered the storm unnecessarily It is because of my lack of knowledge about health and nutrition that I've gone from a size 12 to a size 26, and back and forth in between. I'll let you guess where I am now.

I'll tell you my age, before I tell you my dress size. Talk about being **PROGRAMMED**. That's me.

When it became unacceptable for me to live in a tent, (Yes they still make them) instead of a size that show my curves, it was time to make a change. I never could buy into the myth that extremely large people were comfortable with themselves. There is nothing comfortable about not being able to breath while walking up a flight of stairs, or trying on a dress size that you used to fit, in a fitting room that you can't turn around in.

Fannie Lou Hammer says " When you get sick and tired of being sick and tired, you do something different." I don't recall who, but someone once said, "When you know better, you do better". Hopefully this time, we'll do better, so we don't have to put up with unacceptable acceptance. Now go ahead, and accept that.

Keeping in mind, that not all programming is negative, there are some areas of our lives where programming is necessary, especially if it is to be used constructively. Anytime we personally program ourselves to do something that will enhance the quality of our lives, and it harms no one else, I see nothing wrong with it. Once such young man used programming effectively, and even made a career out of it. That young man is none other than Elroy Smith, Program Director of Chicago's number one radio station, WGCI, 107.5 FM.

Elroy Smith
Program Director
WGCI-FM 107.5
Chicago, Illinois

With the true island flavor of a Bermudan vocalist, Elroy has made, and kept Chicago radio number one in ratings since his arrival. His short lived career as a singer, was truly a blessing in disguise, because his vocal talent helped him blossom into the icon that he is today in the radio industry. Bitten by the entertainment bug in the early 70"s, his voice was recognized by professionals as that of an announcer. He left the islands to attend school in New York, where he studied for nine months, before returning home, and landing a job as a local disc jockey.

His insatiable thirst for knowledge led him to Graham Jr. College in Boston, where he earned his Bachelor's degree in Journalism. He interned at WILD-AM, where he hosted a Caribbean show. Elroy continued his studies at Cambridge College, earning a Masters degree. By 1981 he had worked his way up to full time position. His responsibilities doubled in 1983. He remained an On-Air Personality, but began his stint as the stations Program Director. He moved on to Dallas in 1988 and then to Chicago's number one station, WGCI-FM, in 1992.

Ridding himself of his British Bermudan accent, was one of his greatest challenges, but with the assistance of a professional speech therapist he succeeded.

Obtaining his visa for residence in the United States was another challenge he overcame, with the assistance of the owner of the radio station in which he worked, who provided sponsorship for him to obtain resident alien citizenship status.

One of the many lessons Elroy learned along the way, is to how to develop your own uniqueness, to avoid being seen as just another number. He also suggests something contrary to Corporate America's method of moving up the corporate ladder, and that is not to kiss up. He says, "No matter how powerful the person is that you're talking to, they need to hear your thoughts, your feelings, so don't be afraid to share them." Another management skill he's acquired along the way is not to depend on research as an end to all, it's not the only foolproof system of succeeding. Get to know people, what they do, and help make them better. When you make them better, you become a better person.

He advises others to remember to treat others, as you would want to be treated. When it's all said and done, we all need each other. Treat others with kindness and compassion. He warns newcomers in this business, to concentrate on more than radio, and have a strong back up plan. Planning for the future is an essential part of developing your passion for life. Elroy's passion for the business is self evident. Not only is he number one as the listeners choice, but he's also number one in his church, where he's actually involved in his church ministry. Kind spirits have a tendency to flourish, and his spirit of love and compassion is surely to be recognized where it counts the most.

Most important to remember here, he accepted the fact that he had a British accent, in which he had to get rid of if he wanted to work as a radio personality.

He had many other obstacles to overcome, but he didn't let them stop him. He went to work on a plan to make his dreams become reality. Elroy proved that you don't have to accept any limitations that society put on you. You can carry them around with you forever, or toss them in the trash, where they belong. Now, what's stopping you? Are you allowing your age, your environment, your gender, or circumstances to control your destiny? Excuses are just that. If you look for one, you will always find one. No excuse is acceptable. There's either a *reason or a result*.

Which one have you chosen? Do you have a reason for staying where you are in life, or are you looking for a different result? The choice is yours. You have the gift of choice. Use it wisely. Elroy did, what about you?

Chapter 3

Surrender

"Surrender must take place in us-the giving up of the imperfect to accept the Perfect; the renunciation of the impure to accept the Pure; the abolishment of the personality to be the One.

-Lilian DeWaters,
Light of the Eternal

Every since I can remember, I have always had a problem with people of authority. Anyone who had control over my life, besides me, I had a problem with. It followed me well into my adult life, especially when I was in college. My instructors at Columbia College had warned me. I had heard the all familiar stories, just one too many times. I had even experienced what they had told me, especially from my Introduction to Radio class instructor, who was at that time, in between jobs, but it still didn't seem to sink in. He had been let go of his position as On-Air Talent, (a Radio Personality) at a local radio station, and was teaching part-time at Columbia. He even warned me that my chances were very slim of having any longevity in this business. After all, here was a male, in a male dominated industry, and he was an unemployed jock. He never misled me. He told me point blank that the industry of radio was not particularly open and receptive to women.

This is a male dominated industry. The decision makers are men, and are move apt to hire another man. It's only logical. We do what is expected of us, not going against the normal routine of things.

We wouldn't dare want to step out of our own comfort zone, and hire new talent; someone the public has never heard of. It's the old boy network. Corporate America at it's best. Women seldom begin their careers working prime time, which is mornings or midday, unless they knew someone, or slept with someone. I am not saying that is true of all women, but that is the way it was explained to me. When you're new in the business, you've got to prove yourself. You've got to pay your dues.

You pay your dues by working the shifts that no one else wants. The graveyard shift, 10pm until 2 am, or overnights, 2am until 5am, or 3-6 am, depending on the stations rotation. No one wants to work that shift. Neither did I. Since I didn't know anyone, and wasn't going to sleep with anyone to get prime time, I worked those shifts. I have learned along the way that it's quite pleasant to work those shifts, because it's quite peaceful during those times. No one in the studio but you, the music and your thoughts. Sure, you had the callers who kept you busy, taking requests, ministering to the lonely, sick and shut ins, and your *regulars*. (those who listened to you every single day or night) For the most part, it is an ideal time, especially if you're a loner. Working dayparts, (day shifts) you have to be concerned the constant interruptions of staff, visiting artists, celebrities, etc.

The Continuity department (traffic department, not street traffic, department responsible for the commercial spots played) program changes, difficult callers, all go hand in hand with unexpected interruptions. God forbid you have technical problems that causes *dead air*, (no music) for a few seconds, which feels like an eternity. This is a radio personality's worst nightmare. Dead air means that something is wrong. Seriously wrong.

It means that you're not watching the time, or it could be a simple malfunction of one of the machines.

Whatever the reason is, you will have to report to your immediate supervisor, the Program Director. I assure you, Program Directors are not very happy people when you *consistently* have dead air. It can happen to anyone occasionally, but repeatedly? When this happens, it seems to be a pattern, and that patterns trails behind the person responsible for the act itself. When this continues to happen, they eliminate the problem. You.

What happens to a high profile Radio Personality, who has lost their job and no longer in the public eye? If one is not centered or grounded, this can be a difficult experience. Because this society places value on what we do, instead of who we are, the unemployed has a tendency to feel worthless, when they are no longer gainfully employed. It's very difficult process in any type of unemployment, and very challenging in this type of industry because you're in the public eye.

On the other hand, it can also be a life transforming experience. The in between jobs period, allows you the opportunity to examine where you are in life. If your value is in yourself, not in what you do, the challenge can be less threatening. We get so caught up in what we do, instead on who we are, we forget what is important. What we are on the inside, is far more important that what we do on the outside, on the physical realm. But because we buy into the mindset of the general population, we deny ourselves the opportunity to learn the truth about ourselves, and who we really are. Human beings. *Not Human Doings*.

If you doubt my word, look it up in Webster. Many people cannot except this as truth. We are responsible for our own development and growth. We can blame anyone or anything, but the truth lies within. We can only shift the blame for so long. Blaming someone else for our shortcomings only keeps us in denial, and prevents us from living the quality of life we truly deserve. We are responsible. Always. It's never the other person, or other things that hold us back, or keep us from doing or having whatever it is that we want out of life. It is at this point in life, that we come to this realization, that when we *surrender*, to the Universe, or to our higher power, in which I chose to call God, to the forces that guide us, that we can move forward.

When we give up trying to do things our way, ask for guidance, and allow (have patience) the Universe to guide us to our good, that things begin to fall into place. When we surrender, when we become childlike, (non-judgmental, non expectant, and patient) and allow the forces of nature to guide us, it is at that point that transformation results. Wait. One of the easiest words to remember, in the English language, but one of the most challenging things to do.

My most memorable life transforming experience was my trip to the Motherland for the very first time. I have always wanted to visit Africa, every since grade school, when I learned there was such a place. It wasn't until I was in the downtown Nairobi, Kenya marketplace, that I had an awakening. And that's really what transformation is, an awakening to the truth. Becoming aware, conscious of the truth. Accepting that truth, trusting that truth, and begin to live from that state of enlightened awareness, is truly a transformation.

The transformation came to me in the blinking of any eye. My eyes revealed to me the truth about myself. The truth stood only three feet or so before me, in the human form of a young Kenyan woman, dressed shabbily in American clothing, which was dirty and tattered. She wore a scarf tied around her head, hiding her hair. I immediately thought to myself, "what a shame." What a shame it is to be a native of your own country, and not be adorned in your own native clothing. I couldn't wait to find some unique African outfits to take back home and show my friends and family the real African clothing I bought in Africa. Why would any Afrikkan want to wear American clothing, when they have their own traditional fabric that is so beautiful? Then it hit me. Not like a bolt of lightning, but very gently, like a friend would touch you on the shoulder.

America has such great influence all over the world. Because America and all of it's habits and it's western world ways are so popular, many countries and natives from the continent of Africa want to be recognized as having similar qualities of Americans, and one way show that influence is through fashion, so they wear what Americans wear. At that moment in time, the thought occurred to me, "Oh you poor thing, trying to look like an American, with your American clothing."

Just like I had that thought, another thought flashed in my mind immediately saying, "she's only a reflection of you." I immediately thought to myself, "What? A reflection of myself, how could that be? This lady is nothing like me." As quickly as my defensive answer came, the truth revealed itself to me again. She is exactly like you. The only difference is that she is a native in her homeland, wearing clothing influenced by Americans.

You're an African American living in America, a country does that not recognize or value your worth as a human being, let alone accept you as an American.

The human rights laws are the only reason you are allowed to live in America, and those rights are being challenged. Here you are, blessed with a privilege to visit the Motherland, in which multitudes will never see. Here you are visiting your native continent, unsure of which part of Africa your ancestors were taken from during enslavement, who survived the Diaspora, and you have the audacity to judge a native. Chances are she knows from whence she came, or at least knows what tribe she her ancestors came from. Do you? I was stunned as those embarrassing thoughts whirled around inside my mind. How dare I? How dare I think such thoughts? I was startled at the order and the amount of thoughts that were ramshacking my mind, in only a fraction of a few seconds.

I was so anxious to buy any fabric that was of Afrikkan origin that I could take back home, that would somehow keep me connected, and continuously remind me of my Afrikkaness. I wanted to run out of my mind and into the nearest shop to find fabric, so that my mind would stop talking to me, but I couldn't. Her smile wouldn't let me. I smiled back at her, as I always do, to strangers or loved ones, and offered her my heart. Not one single word was uttered between the two of us. Only our eyes, our hearts, and the spirits of our ancestors were with us. It was if I was standing on holy ground. Her mere presence had taught me a very valuable lesson, one that I probably would never have experienced in an institution of higher learning. For that experience, I was most grateful. I offered her a Kenyan shilling, she accepted, and we parted ways. My education in the act of surrendering was in full force. Tuition paid in full.

I'm not saying that your experience on the act of surrendering, has to be so dramatic, but what I am saying is that you should try and be open to the process itself. Now I could have very well been arrogant about it and shoved those thoughts in the back of my mind, and continued my shopping spree without giving that woman a second thought. But because I was there on a spiritual journey, waiting to have an experience of some kind, I allowed the experience to happen through me, rather than fight it. My idea of her being a pitiful person, would have only kept me trapped in thoughts of lack and limitation. I would have not been able to see the whole picture. She was perfect, whole and complete, just as she was. My thoughts about her appearance did not make her any less of an Africkkan, a Kenyan, a woman, or any other thing.

When I opened my mind, and allowed the truth to filter in, it was at that point in time, I was freed from my own judgments. To quote Cinque, from the movie Amistad, as he stood shackled by the neck and wrists saying, "Let Us Free". It's up to us to free ourselves, by allowing the process of surrender, to move, think, and have it's being, in, through, and around us. When we surrender to our higher power, and ask for daily guidance, then we will be free. It is only the thoughts of lack and limitation that keep us imprisoned. Free yourself.

Try this exercise. Put the book down, and think for just a few minutes, about something that you are having a challenge with. It could be a relationship with family, co-workers, or some authority figure. Maybe it's your finances. There never seems to be enough to meet your needs. Too much month at the end of your money? Maybe it's your job that has you stressed out. Your children are not living up to your expectations, bad grades, hanging out with the wrong crowd? What about your health? Are you eating the kinds of live foods that give you energy, and make you feel good, or do you do what most of us do, and eat whatever is most convenient? Do you workout, walk a mile a day, or do something to sweat out the toxins you intake daily? Is your spouse, partner, better half, other half, or significant other not satisfying your needs? Are you unhappy with some part of your life? If so, then be sure and try out this exercise. Read the whole exercise before you try it.

- **Get somewhere quiet where you won't be disturbed.**
- **(Try a dark room, sitting in a comfortable chair where you can relax your body.)**
- **Close you eyes, and take several lonnnnnnng, deeeeeeeeepth, breaths.**
- **Inhale and exhale through your nostrils, with your mouth closed.**
- **Focus on your breathing and nothing else. Feel your stomach inflate,**
  and deflate, as you breath in and out.
- **Take about 10 (ten) l-o-n-g, d-e-e-p breaths,**

Ask yourself this question.

What is it that I can do to make this situation better?

Then repeat this affirmation to yourself, several times, or as many times as you feel it necessary.

- *I RELEASE, AND LET GO.*

Be patient and wait for an answer. Continue breathing.

Ask the question again, if no answer is revealed.

Part of the surrendering process is learning patience. I know it's not easy in this microwave world in which we live, but remember, Rome wasn't built in a day.

Sometimes answers come right away, sometimes they take longer. Sometimes the answer is to just be, not having to do anything. We live in a society that values doing, more than being, so we have to adjust ourselves accordingly. Sometimes we just need to sit still, and be alone with our thoughts. There is so much that demands our time, we can't hear our inner voice speaking to us because of all the noise that surrounds us.

We must quite ourselves. Only then can we hear. To sum the results up in a short sentence, I share with you a quoted from The Wisdom of the Taoists, which says, "No one can see their reflection in running water. It is only in still water can we see."

Try this act of surrendering daily. Spend a few minutes in the morning before you start your day. throughout the day, when you find yourself in a situation in which things are not going as you planned, or as you would like them to, simply STOP, and practice the act of SURRENDER. Notice the difference it will make in the quality of the decisions you make throughout the day. Simply LET GO! The Universal plan has already been established. The way has already been made. Your reluctance to it is what stops you. Simply go! Don't try to do everything you planned, your way.

Sometimes things happen the way they do so that we can have the experience of seeing how it could very well be okay another way. Remember to make surrendering a part of your day, and slowly recognize the blessings that will occur as a result of practicing the art of surrender. Until we take the time to quiet ourselves and go within, we prolong enjoying the blessings that await us. We're too busy to listen to the inner voice.

Surrendering can come in many forms. Sometime it could mean letting go of someone, or something you're physically attached to. It's those physical attachments to things, that keep us in bondage, in some form or another. Don't let any THING, stand between you and what you have been assigned to do. Step out on faith. Letting go is never easy, but it can be done. Just ask Hermene Hartman, Publisher of N'DIGO Magazine. She gave up her prized possession to launch her own business.

Hermene Hartman
Publisher
N'DIGO Magazine

As a seasoned journalist, she is constantly aware of the poor news coverage of African Americans. Hermene says, "It is not representative of who we are as a people. It is not what I call full measure. You see the bad guys, the burglar, the robber, the gang bangers. You see us portrayed negatively, less than what we are, and not *who* we are."

It disturbed her that she did not see a businessmen, a college graduate, or a good kid, portrayed in the news. It disturbed her that she didn't see people like you and I, who go to work everyday, pay taxes, go to church, and send their kids to school. That kind of person was missing. Before she began her own publication, Hermene said, "I didn't see Black reality being covered. Not that the robber doesn't rob, or that the gang bangers don't exist, but that is not all of us, as a people. I saw it as a misrepresentation, and I wanted to create a product that would present us as *full measured,* not just as a people with problems."

The other thing that bothered her the was the way in which black folks were put in a minority box. It was a very *niggerish* portrayal, not as a full American citizen, living the American dream. Hermene wanted that stereotypical image to change, and the only way it was going to change, was to do something about it. And she did.

Not only did her homework of starting a publication include the regular route of research, examining various types of magazines and newspapers locally, she even traveled abroad. In Europe, she walked the streets studying what papers moved, which ones didn't, and why. She says she even walked up to people on the street and asked them why they bought a particular paper.

She repeatedly received the same reply when asking people why they chose to read one publication over another. She says, "What I heard everybody saying was, we like color, we like pictures. The front pages of papers don't have pictures. When I took that information back for analysis, they said it simply doesn't happen. Well today, every paper in Chicago has a picture on it. If they have money, guess what kind of picture they have on it? Color. I recognized that this society has changed from a literal society to a visual society, with the invent of television, videos and the personal computer, we see a picture before we read. I was seeing that. My intuition told me that. I was recognizing the change, while many others were not."

A portion of that research also led her to not rely solely on the opinions offered by the experts. She went beyond the normal way of doing things, and went directly to her market, to the people who would read her publication. She explains, "We were trying to capture people where they play, where they work, and where they pray. Those were our criteria. I would ask a person, *Where do you go?* You go to work, you go to church, and you go somewhere to play, and *play* is a big category. You go to the health club, to restaurant, the park, and to the club".

Reaching people where they frequent most, was a major concern in distribution. Even distribution was a little different than the norm. In their first distribution, they used a different approach, using some non-traditional outlets. Hermene smiles as she adds, "We're in churches. Nobody puts papers in churches." That is, nobody, until N'DIGO started doing it.

Hermene knew that if she could capture you in one of those places, then she had a shot at you. If she captured you at all three of those places, she was on your radar screen. That was her mode of distribution. She admits that when she first started, people told her she was out of her mind. But she knew this was where people traffic, and that she was not out of her mind. She knew with all her heart and soul, that it was going to work, and it did.

N'DIGO has grown from monthly, to bi-monthly, and is celebrating May of this year, as the first full year as a *weekly* publication. On starting a new business, Hermene explains, "The challenges have been what every small business goes through. Establishing yourself in the market place, capitalization, selling advertising, hiring and maintaining good, solid, and reliable staff, is a concern. Not to mention acceptance in an industry where the market place is full. She adds, "I was told that what I was doing was not the way its done. They said I was crazy. I knew I wasn't crazy, and I knew it could be done."

Under the guidance of Hermene, N'DIGO has overcame the obstacles, and done some non traditional things in the newspaper printing industry, such as color, on the cover of the paper, with a photograph. She created something what she calls a *magapaper,* which is a magazine format on news print. That in itself was non traditional. You either created a magazine or a newspaper, period. Hermene combined the two, adding to the success of N'DIGO, as *the* urbane publication to read.

N'DIGO not only gives a positive portrayal of African Americans, but you actually see the people on the cover. These people live in the community. You see them at church, as well as social events, and know that these people are real, and they really do exist. It provides hope, whereas the daily publications usually don't. Since we live in a visual society, these photographs and stories, remind us of the possibilities, and empowers us to strive more. These photographs are vital to the survival, not only to the paper, but to us as a people.

Being in business for yourself demands commitment, hard work, and trusting your gut feeling. It was intuition that drove her to start from a bootstrap operation. She never took out a loan, didn't qualify for the SBA loan, (Small Businessman's Association) or any of that stuff. She started from scratch in the beginning. Plain and simple. If you placed an add, you paid for it. Hermene adds, "We've had remarkable growth. I relied on the experts for some information, but I relied on my market for my direction, because I knew that this was missing in the market place and, I wasn't the only one feeling that. From day one, when we hit the streets, we've never had enough copies, to this day we still don't." Hermene adds, "The demand is overwhelming. I look at it as a new company with a new product coming to the market. Be it a big company or a small one, those are just some of the things you run up against. Like any other business, such as Ted Turner or Bill Gates, anything new is perceived with caution.

Could you imagine Bill Gates telling someone that he was going to put a little TV screen on your desk with a little typing apparatus with it, and change the whole world of business? Can you imagine that? They probably would have locked him up. Can you imagine Ted Turner saying something like, "I don't like the way you all do news, there's another way to do it. I'm not even going to use big name anchor people, I'm just going to play on people in their locals, all over the world. People thought he was crazy. That's not the way you do news. They thought he was mad."

Hermene admits it herself, "I saw the news business as kind of old, stagnated, out of touch with the way people really are, which was based on customer research information I received from my customers. I relied on this information, as opposed to the *experts*. I did rely on the experts for business because there are some firm rules of business that must be adhered to that are permanent. I listened to what the experts, and what my customer base was saying, but most of all I had to listen to myself. I call that *selective* listening.

For those interested in starting their own business, be it a magazine or anything else, she shares her expertise saying that, "It is important to know your market, and have a whole lot of energy. Business is ruthless. Business is hard. It's beyond a good idea. The question is, do you have the energy to pull the idea off? Do you have commitment, the dedication to do what you've got to do to make it happen? Rely on yourself and nobody else. Ideas are a dime a dozen. It's not that it's not a good idea, everybody you know has a good idea, but are you committed to the idea? Can you make the idea come alive? It's kind of like someone saying, I want to have a baby. But do you want to get pregnant? Do you really want to raise the child? You need to think through those issues. Being in the publishing business is a highly competitive business, and requires stamina, but it it's also a business that is filled with opportunities.

Suppose someone told you ten years ago that you would be receiving your news on something called *on line*, and that you would be able to communicate all over the world. You would have put them away. Yahoo proved them wrong. She laughs as she says, "Who would've believed that a portion of our workforce would be at home, on a computer? The breakthroughs are coming through every single day. Who would have believed cable TV might out do the major stations? That's what I mean by opportunities available.

It's the technology, which allows you to really do some things, to be creative, to stretch, and imagine, and perform. She leaves us with a final thought, and that is, to believe in yourself, be willing to work extra hard, and trust your gut feeling."

N'DIGO is *proof in the pudding*, that one can begin an idea, follow it up with action, and make your dreams come true. I will always remember hearing about the genesis of N'DIGO, when Hermene was the keynote speaker at Women Employed's Anniversary in 1997. She told the story of how she sold her prized possession, a classic BMW, to purchase a computer to write her first story. That my friend, is passion, coupled with purpose. What are you willing to give up, in order to get what you want?

Chapter 4

Setting Priorities

"Things which matter most
must never be at the mercy
of things which matter the least."
-Goethe

How many times have we sat down, and written out goals that we never keep? How many times have we written down goals that we had no intentions of keeping? How many times have we taken the time to write down a goal because someone suggested it, Like Oprah's Gratitude Journal, but our hearts just weren't in it? Sound familiar? Well, don't feel bad about it, and beat up on yourself, society will do enough of that for you. The most important thing here is to recognize it, and move forward.

Prioritize. First things first Take ownership. Own whatever it is that you do, BEFORE you begin the process. It's like making a major purchase in your life, like buying a home. You wouldn't save your hard earned money for five years in a row, eating brown bag lunches, missing after work cocktails with your co-workers, missing your weekly visits to the barbershop, manicurist, massage therapist, or whatever simple pleasures that you indulge in, to allow some stranger to move in to your new home with your down payment, now would you?

Then why allow something as simple as a goal, to cause chaos and wreck havoc in your life? Make sure that this is something that you, and you alone, want you to do. Take the time and ask yourself a few simple, but life altering questions. Why? Why am I doing this?

What significant difference will it make in the quality of my life, and those around me? If you can't honestly answer these questions, then maybe you should ask yourself this question. Who's voice is it in the back of my head, that says I need to do this? Are there demands on me from those around me? Is there peer pressure? Does my supervisor, manager, co-worker, partner, lover, child, in-laws or anyone else beside me, expect this of me? We have to take the time out to identify where that voice comes from. Could it be the voice of an old teacher who subliminally suggested that you achieve this goal, and since you haven't until this date done it, you feel that you have failed?

Could it possibly be that voice? Oh No! It couldn't possibly be Mrs. Hatchell, (may her soul rest in peace) who told me that I should major in English or Literature, because of my good grades? Oh that could not possibly be. I hated English. It's not my fault I was so good at it. I just liked to write, and spelling was a part of that. I couldn't be a very good writer if I couldn't spell good. I didn't try to be good at it on purpose. I just didn't like math.

I remember seeing my mother write a note to the teacher for me to take to school one day. I thought to myself, that sure is some fancy writing. I sure wish I could write like that. It was like a secret society. My teacher would give me notes to take home to my mom to read, in a sealed envelope. I would be tempted to try and open it, without her ever knowing it.

Like they did on the Perry Mason show, where the lady was trying to steam open the envelope to read the letter that came in the mail for her husband who was cheating on her, but she just couldn't prove it.

She couldn't get the envelope open either. Neither could I. Besides, I didn't know how to make steam. The only steam I ever saw, came out of the radiator, and I couldn't wait until winter to come for the janitors to turn on the steam heat. So I never got to see what was in those sealed envelopes.
But I sure could imagine. And that is exactly what I did. I begin to write my own secret notes to myself, in my writing tablet, just like I was the teacher, and the momma too. That is where my passion for writing began. Those precious moments of memories past are still with me today, even as I write this book.

The memories of Momma and Mrs. Hatchell. What I remember about Mrs. Hatchell the most, is that she always wore the same outfit two days in a row. She said it didn't make sense to clean it after wearing it only one time.

Have you taken a trip down memory lane, and visited your voices of the past? If not, then take a few minutes and reminisce. You might recognize a face, or a voice or two. That's the purpose of the experience, to get in touch with the part of you that wants to set this goal in the first place. Once you can own the goal, know that it is yours, something that you want to do because YOU want to do it, then it will become a part of you. It will be a priority. It will allow you to rise to the occasion to do it. It will become realistic, because you set it. Not someone from your past, present, or future, but you and you alone want to achieve this thing.

This something that adds meaning to your life, this thing that brings joy to your being. This goal. This priority. This thing that makes you eager to stay up late at night, miss family, friends, and events, and still wake up refreshed the next morning, ready to take on the day's challenges.

One of the greatest challenges is to figure out what is a realistic goal. Common sense tells us that we can't do certain things, like get a graduate degree, (because no one else in the family has done it) go on and become president of some company. Or better yet, we can't become an entrepreneur, until we develop the discipline necessary to run a successfully business. You can not be an entrepreneur, and not get along with people. You won't make friends, establish healthy business relationships, or make money by not returning phone calls, or showing up at appointments.

Common sense would also tells us that once we identify the goal, we make the determination as to whether we can accomplish the goal. We cannot allow outside circumstances or situations determine for us whether or not this is a realistic goal or not. Sometimes it's better to leave common sense on the back burner for a while. What is realistic to me , may not be realistic to you. It's all a matter of choice. Take the time and make the decision as to what is a realistic goal in each area of your life. We often get so caught up in the area of working, and making money, being successful, that we neglect all the other areas of our lives that make us whole. In addition to our career, there are six other areas of equal importance. (Other areas of equal importance are spiritual, mental, physical, educational, family, and social.)

Our spirituality is the most important, but most neglected until there is chaos or tragedy in our lives before we get in tune with it. Our spiritual goals are the goals that guide us through the maze of mass and confusion in times of turmoil. Once we have taken the time to establish what those goals are, it is not to say that at some point in time you won't be shaken from the root of your very existence, but you will have a foundation to fall back on. Something reserved within you will give you the resiliency to forge ahead when nothing seems to be working. Our spirituality is the core of who we are. It is the essence of our being.

You can't be anything less than what you already are, and you are a spiritual being, whether you recognize it or not. Spirit does not force itself on you. Spirit awaits your acceptance of it. Spirit is you. You are spirit! You are simply a spiritual being, enclosed in human form, having a human experience. The experiences we have are only for the sake of teaching us to grow. Our body, is the vehicle, by which we experience life.

As we grow spiritually, we open ourselves to the possibilities, and set new priorities, based on our acceptance of who and what we are as spiritual entities. Now, what is the one thing that you have placed on the back burner that you would really like to accomplish? Take a moment, and write it here.

My number one priority is:

____

(Don't turn the page until you complete this sentence.)

Is it a priority that you truly desire, that will enhance the quality of your life, as well as those around you? If not, why not? If this *thing*, is not a burning desire deep from within, then maybe you better re-think your position, as to the real reason why you want to achieve it. If it is only to make more money, to buy more things, that keep you and your credit, in bondage, and sacrifices your soul. Ask yourself the question, is it really worth it? If it is, at what cost? Your health? Your job or career? Your relationships?

Isn't it funny how we didn't know that we were poor, until we were adults? We didn't know that we were considered as living in poverty, until we read about in the newspaper, or heard it on the television or radio. After all this time, (now that we're all grown up) it's still amazing how we let other people, inform us as to how good or bad we are doing. We still don't live in the *right* neighbor-hood, drive *the* right car, not married to *the* right spouse, don't have the *right* political connections, *the* degree, have that high stressed to the limit, high powered position, that we know we *deserve*, have 2.5 kids, or take that two week vacation in the Cayman Islands. We don't have any of that stuff that *they* say that we need, and are then made to feel bad about because we don't have any of it.

Ever stopped to think about it for a moment? Ask yourself the question. Who are *they*? Why is what *they* say, so important? Why do I value what *they* say, over what *I* think? Why? Why? Who's in control of me, and my thoughts? Me? They? Who? Is the depth of my programming so conditioned, that I don't even bother to think for myself? Wow! Could this be true? It has to be, after all, *they* have everything, so it has to be true.

They *(the experts)* also have all the HMO's, PPO's, and the highest OD (overdose) rates to coincide with all the ulcers, heart bypasses, migraine headaches, divorce rates, suicides, genocide. Don't forget about the addictions, the affairs, the lost of integrity, shame, confusion, anger, and a host of other ailments to go along with everything else *they* deem as necessary to live a certain quality of life.

The question is, whose quality of life? Whose life are we talking about here? My life or theirs? After all, isn't it unrealistic to have anything but what they say is the best? Realistically speaking, I shouldn't have anything. It just isn't realistic. What is really unrealistic, is the fact that we buy into this human race consciousness, of lack, limitation, disease, and poverty. So why not take it a step further, and dream some unrealistic dreams. Everything else is unrealistic, so why stop here? Let's go all the way. Let's dream dreams that no man could ever accomplish. Especially someone from where I come from. That way, if we don't reach the highest goal that we originally set for ourselves, at least we went beyond the point of reality. It's only reality, if we think it to be so.

It's only unrealistic, if we think so. We are the ones who count. We all have individual dreams. No one can dream our dreams for us. NO one can think our thoughts for us. No one can make our reality. We do it all by ourselves.

Now that is not to say that we may not have some assistance along the way. We might take a course or two, here and there. We might even obtain a degree or two, or three. Who's counting? We might even indulge in a process known as creative visualization, where we can really open up our minds, and let our imagination run wild.

We can imagine ourselves, as having all our needs and desires abundantly fulfilled. And why not? It is realistic. Or is it? Says who? What may be reality for one person, is not necessarily the same for the next.

So let's step out of the reality mode, and into the mode of being unrealistic. Aim so high, in your spirituality, that when things come falling down, all around you, you won't be damaged by the rainfall. Aim high in your quest for spirituality, and everything else just seems to fall into place. Aim so unrealistically high, in your quest to discover your purpose in life, one that is pleasing to the maker, most high, and watch what once seemed to be unrealistic, become realistic. Don't think it's possible? Maybe you should read Les Brown's book, Live Your Dreams. By all means, listen to the audio cassette, It's Possible.

When you begin to see the possibilities, then you can believe it. We have to learn to see with the minds eye, the eye of faith, not the human eye. As my powerful sister, Iyanla Vanzant said at the 1996 African American Women on Tour Conference in Chicago, "Don't let those lying eyes fool you". Realistically speaking, it's very unrealistic, and contrary to the laws of the nature, to think that you cannot accomplish any goal you set forth do, as long as it is in harmony with Universal Law. All really is well. So go ahead and set those goals high, where they belong. The Universe awaits your decision. Don't wait too long. You know *they* will be doubting you all the way, and you don't want to prove them right, now do you?

They will always try to make us feel inadequate, because *they* don't believe they can accomplish their goals, if they have any. That's why they tell us that we can't do it. Congressman Jesse Jackson, Jr., proved them all wrong.

Jesse Jackson, Jr.
Congressman
Illinois

Since he was old enough to make a conscious decision about the what course his life would take, Congressman Jesse Jackson, Jr. has clearly demonstrated that goals are the key to moving forward in life. Having been exposed at an early age, he has always been interested in public service, even though he was not sure what form that public service would take. He attended Chicago Theological Seminary, and University of Illinois College of Law. After graduation he had to decide what area he could best serve in. He did not know if it would be in the ministry, or representing peoples interest before the bar, but he did know that it would be in the service capacity.

The opportunity presented itself for him to serve in Congress, and he genuinely believes that it is in positions of government power, that one is in a position to distribute resources to help feed people, and provide education for them. Congressman Jackson says, "That's his true passion." The community knows that shares that sentiment as well, that he has definitely made a difference in his district, on the far south side of Chicago. Although the challenges have been many, one of his greatest challenges was being accepted into the political arena.

As a candidate for congress, some said he was too young. Congressman Jackson said, "I looked at the constitution, it said I had to be twenty five years old, and I was thirty one years old, so I knew I met that constitutional qualification.

I thought about the contribution of Martin Luther King, Jr., who departed this life at thirty five, and Malcolm x who was gone at age thirty nine, and I thought about the contribution of Jesus the Christ who was on Calgary at age thirty three. So I said to myself if a Kennedy can be in congress at age twenty six, why can't I be in congress at age thirty one? So I quickly overcame in my own mind, the age barrier." There were some concerns about youthfulness and, lack of experience. He adds, having grown up in my parents household and the exposure that I had, I felt relatively comfortable in terms of the issue of inexperience. That which I didn't know, I would quickly learn."

He openly admits that other obstacles, such as the obstacles of the institution itself, makes it a daily challenge. It's a seniority based system and going in as a freshman, it takes time to gain seniority. Fortunately, he's young enough to get seniority in due time. He humbly admits that "It's just a function of recalibrating my attitude so that I can be patient enough, and that's what I've been working on."

In setting one's priorities, he's the first to eloquently say that one should have a commitment, and a calling that is higher than ones personal ambition "My father always told me that to be a lawyer is not enough. Don't become a lawyer just because you want a car, a nice house, or you want a better quality of life for yourself. Become a lawyer because people are in genuine need of justice, and in genuine need of fairness. In other words, *seek ye first the kingdom of God*, and all other things will be added. In due time, you'll get money, but gain experience and have a genuine commitment to help people who cannot help themselves. As long as people need help, and trust me, he said, there will be people who will always need help, you will always be in a position to help them, if people believe you genuinely want to help them."

Rev. Jesse Jackson Jr. said the same thing about medical doctors. He said, don't become a doctor just because you want a nice house or a nice car, or a nice watch. You become a doctor because people are sick, and people have illnesses, and affirmatives, and they need assistance. If you discover the cure for aids or cancer because you have a genuine passion to wipe out a human illness, all other things, including money and car, and wealth and things will be added unto that. In other words, *don't lose your sense of purpose*. Again, *seek ye first the kingdom.*

For those who aspire to have a political career, he advises, "Don't just look at what I do, say hey I want to be a Congressman one day. I could live without the title, I could even live without the job. It's my passion for what I do and what I want to accomplish, not as an answer to myself, but to answer the prayer of every Amistad African who was on that ship, who longed for representation, and someone who would argue their case on the floor of the congress about the kind of tyranny that occurred at that time."

"I see myself as others see themselves as part of the fulfillment of a three hundred and seventy nine year proposition, in America. And so in lining our own ambitions with history, and trying to determine where we are aging, and where we should be going well help provide the kind of clarity we need for this hour."

Congressman Jackson continues to be a shining example, of when you pray and ask for knowledge, wisdom, and understanding about the direction in which you should follow, your true purpose will unfold.

Once you make up in your mind, a set of realistic priorities that you can achieve, nothing will stop you, except you. Have you taken the time to put your priorities in order? If not, why not? The world awaits your contribution, because only you can give, what you came here to give.

And he's been giving since he first stepped into office. His record speaks for itself. Let the record show, his contributions continue to make a difference in the community, and the world. Congressman Jackson is no different than you or I. He had a plan, and stuck to it. He didn't allow them to disuade him from reaching his goals. Can you say the same?

Chapter 5

Inventory

"Each of us has a center, though we usually don't recognize it as such. Neither do we recognize the all-encompassing effects of that center on every aspect of our lives."

-Stephen Covey
The 7 Habits Of Highly Effective People

Every single thought, feeling, or emotion we have ever had is recorded in the cell membranes of our bodies. Many of those experiences have been joyful ones. Some of those experiences we would rather not be reminded of. It is those experiences, the painful ones, that sometime govern our lives. This is the reason why personal inventory is so very, very, important. Now, I will not say that this will be easy, as a matter of fact, it is one of the most difficult things you will ever have to do in your life. The pure satisfaction of the self discovery process outweighs the pain. If you doubt me, try this exercise.

Remember the time when you:

- experienced your most embarrassing moment?

- had to speak in front of an audience and you went blank?

- acknowledged you had a serious problem and sought help?

- Decided to seek help, but backed out?
- The time you lied, got caught, and had to fess up?
- you cut yourself so bad, you had to have stitches?
- You broke a limb, and had to have a cast?
- you had surgery, and recovery was so painful?
- Lost a loved one?
- Separated?
- Someone left you without any warning?
- Received divorce papers?
- Experienced Excruciating labor pains?
- Did your kids homework, and they failed the class anyway?
- Not having enough money to…?
- Wrote a bad check?
- Wrote a proposal, and watched a co-worker get credit for it?
- Got blamed for something someone else did?

Watched authorities repossess your car, and said it was stolen?

Got fired, demoted, looked over for a promotion?

Lied on an application, and got caught?

Watched someone in need and did nothing about it?

Treated unfairly?

Reflection

Now that you've had some time to reflect, all sorts of thoughts are zooming around in your mind. And that's good. When you identified with any of those situations, can you remember what area of your life you were most concerned with at that point in time? What was your main focus? What area of your life did you give the most attention to, and less to the others? Oftentimes we are so caught up in the drama of the moment, we forget who we really are, and the power within us to overcome any circumstance. We are so mesmerized by the moment that our *center*, the core of who we really are, is temporarily thrown off. This imbalance is an opportunity to learn how to center yourself in the midst of confronting an issue. The challenge sometimes is to call attention to the other areas in your life that is lacking, that needs your attention.

When you are *centered* in the area of which your focus is on, something or someone else suffers. The idea of centering, is to provide a balance in all areas of your life, so that there will be a smooth flow of your life, and your daily experiences. One sure way to provide that delicate balance is to find out what is most important to you, and even more importantly, why?

This is where you begin the process of taking your own personal inventory, just as you would take inventory of what there is in the refrigerator, so you don't buy the same things when you go to the grocery store. You'd probably buy cereal and milk if you already had them, would you? You wouldn't pack wool suits if you're headed to the Bahamas would you? So why wait until you have crisis after crisis, before you decide to take inventory of your life, to see where you can make life more enjoyable for yourself and your family.

I can remember one relationship I was involved in that served many of my physical needs, but provided nothing in the area of my emotional needs. After several years, I decided that what I was receiving from this relationship was not worth it, simply because my emotional needs were not being fulfilled.
It was okay, or rather, I simply accepted it in the beginning because I had other immediate needs that were more important.

Well, as time changes, so do people and their needs. Everyone goes through physical, mental and emotional phases. What once worked for me then, may not work for me four or five years later. Neither will it for you. This is why it is vital to your growth and development to stop and take time to write down what is most important in your life, and the next most important, down to the least important. Prioritize.

Someone who is a workaholic, denies him/herself the opportunity to experience life fully because they are so caught up in the process of being what society has termed "successful."

Others are caught in the assumption that money is the answer. Yes, money does provide for our creature comforts, but it does not provide warmth, and the love that we all need to live in this world.

Those who say otherwise, are simply in denial. It's okay to be in denial, as long as you don't stay there. Denial is part of the recovery process. Denial is healthy, as long as you move on. Many people get stuck in denial, and never get out. Personal inventory can help you recognize it for what it is. Recognizing that something is not working in your life, and taking action to make an effective change is part of the process. It does no good to complain about it to people who can do nothing about it.

During my late twenties, I was becoming increasingly uncomfortable in the types of jobs I was working. I did mostly clerical and reception work, and become so efficient at it, that it was no longer a challenge. So once I became bored, I would look for another position at another company, doing the same thing.

Well, once I mastered that job, I was bored again and on to looking for the next job. I always thought that something was wrong with me that I would only stay on a job for a year of so. It never dawned on me that there was nothing *wrong* with me, as a matter of fact, it was exactly *right*, for me to feel that way. It was Spirit trying to express through me, that I had bigger and better things to do. Not to say that clerical work is unimportant, because it is vital to the success of any business. It was simply my time to move on. I had needed those clerical skills I had acquired that would prepare me for my careers in radio broadcasting and public speaking.

Those positions served me well. They allowed me the opportunity to learn how to handle difficult people, and how to interact with all kinds of people of different socio-economic backgrounds. Once I made a decision to do something different, by going back to school to study radio broadcasting, I felt better about myself, and my life. But first, I had to come to the realization that clerical work was not something I wanted to retire from. So I had to come up with a plan that would allow me to do something different than what I was presently doing.

My inventory disclosed the fact that although I knew that my voice was my talent, I didn't know yet just how to get where I wanted to be in life. Your inventory will allow you to discover things about yourself that you may not be aware of, and something you're already aware of, that could possibly make a dramatic difference in the quality of life that you're living.

I suggest that you sit down with pen and paper, (it's important to see it in print because our minds work on the visual plane. Our minds see pictures. Once those thoughts are down on paper, this is where the process of creative visualization occurs. Your personal computer, voicemail, a small recorder, a mastermind partner, or whatever works for you will do. What method you use is the least important. The fact that you take the time to take your personal inventory is of more importance.

Write down the following:

- What areas of your life work well?

1.______________________________

2.______________________________

3.______________________________

4.______________________________

5.______________________________

- Which areas could use improvement?

1.______________________________

2.______________________________

3.______________________________

4.______________________________

5.______________________________

- **What is your purpose in this life? Why are you here?**

Let's take a look at all the areas of our lives.

Financial

Is making money your sole purpose in life? Is there nothing more important? To what lengths will you go to get? Will you do illegal things, or things that are out of character, that jeopardize your health and well being of yourself and you family? Will you stop at no cost to get it? If this is the case, you might want to ask yourself why? Where did you get the idea that the more money that you have, the better or easier your life will be?

I cannot deny that an abundance of money sure helps make life more comfortable, but it is not the key to a happy life. People with lots of money have lots of problems just like people with little or no money. You say you'd rather have lots of money and then you'll deal with the problems when they get there. Millionaires, especially new millionaires, will attest to the problems they encountered upon receiving large sums of money

Relatives come out of nowhere, and enemies become friends. Money brings along it's own set of problems. Where did you develop the concept that you presently have about money? Was it learned in school, at home, in the neighborhood? If you were anything like most kids, you learned along the way. You watched your parents or grandparents.

You probably never took any money management courses, but you were expected to know how to effectively handle money without any course on how to. Bankruptcy court is a good indication of that, not to mention all the unpaid debts, that lead up to the national debt.

Don't the TV ads about getting out of debt via bankruptcy or chapter 13 simply irk you? They encourage folks not to be financially responsible. Until we heal our relationship with money, we will always have money problems, even though it may seem like we don't. There's a powerful audio cassette program by Joe Dominquez, who has passed on, but left a powerful message behind with a six audio cassette program entitled,

Healing Your Relationship With Money,
Achieving Financial Independence".
Contact Information:
New Road Map Foundation
P.O. BOX 15981, Seattle, Washington
98115.

Career

What about your work life? Are you a workaholic? Do you drown yourself in your work and neglect those most dear to you? Do your children really know you? Is your family life in such a shambles that you don't even have a clue as to how to begin to put the pieces back together?

Do you forget and miss birthdays, anniversaries, special occasions? What is so disturbing in your family or personal life that you would rather spend more time at work, than handle the challenges of your family life, that make this world what it is today?

What unresolved issues from childhood have you not dealt with yet? You wonder why your kids don't respect you. You wonder why teens are killing teens. Homicide is at an all time high. Crime and drugs are rampant. You wonder why the world is in the shape it's in, because we are so busy working, to provide a comfortable life, but at what cost. You can drive a nice car, but how long before someone tries to take it from you. You're so buried in your work, you can't see what's coming.

Material Possessions

What are you working for? To buy more things, to make you happy? When you get tired of those things, you buy more things. With the rate of modern technology, you'll run out of money before you could possibly keep up with every new gadget on the market.

Gallagher, a popular comedian sums it all up. He says, "Even if you don't buy every new item advertised, you probably need somewhere to put the stuff you bought. Some of it probably has to be insured, so that if someone takes it from you, you can get some more. When you run out of room, you go and rent storage space, or buy another house, or add on another room, just so you'll have room for all the stuff you've bought. You can only use so much stuff.

After a while, you have so much stuff, you have to have garage sales or give it away." It would seem more logical to just save more money, buy less stuff, and save yourself the hassle of trying to find room to put it. How illogical would that be?

Friends/Associates

Who are you trying to impress anyway? The people you're trying to impress with all your stuff, have their own stuff to deal with. They're too busy trying to find a place to put their stuff, they don't even notice your stuff, not until you mention it, or show up in it. They could care less.

They're up to there credit card limits just like the rest. Real friends don't want your stuff, they want something much more than stuff. They want something only you can give them. They want you. They want your time, your energy, your conversation. They want a part of you, that stuff, or a gift cannot give them.

Family

You can only give your family so much stuff. What they really want, is your time and attention. Are you fulfilling your family's needs? Do you spend quality time? Do you spend time talking about the day's events? Do you eat dinner together? Do you play with the children? Do you visit relatives who can't get out and do for themselves, If not, why not? Family is one of the reasons we all exists.

If it were not for family, we probably wouldn't be here. We didn't get here on our own, we had some help.

Spirituality

Do you spend all your time helping everyone else, before taking care of your own spiritual, mental, and physical needs? Do you tend more to your family's needs, neglecting yourself? You come first. Do you spend more time working at the church, than you do on yourself? If your life is centered around the church, be sure that you don't neglect your responsibilities at home. There has to be a balance. That's what spirituality is all about, providing a balance.

Husband/Wife/Significant Other

Many people make the mistake of putting their partners needs before their own. There's nothing wrong with attending to the needs of your loved ones, but not before your own. What makes it okay, to tend to someone else's needs before taking care of self first? Where did you learn that? Probably from your grandparents, when all grandma had to do was take care of grandpa because he was the breadwinner. But long before grandma took care of grandpa, she had to be sure she took care of self, so she could take care of grandpa. She couldn't very well take care of anyone if she was sick, now could she?

Well, nothing has changed. We must take care of ourselves first, in order to provide for the needs of our loved ones. Now if that means putting something or someone on hold for a little while, then so be it. Self preservation is the first law of nature.

Self

Now that does not mean that one has to be self centered, that the world has to evolve around you, because it does not, even though it may appear to be. Life is constantly changing. The world is constantly changing. If who you are, or what you do, is what makes your world what it is, you're in for a big surprise. Since nothing remains the same. Your self centeredness cannot remain in tact forever. The world evolves around those who evolve around it.

We're all in this together, so we must work together, not independently, but interdependently. No man is an island to himself. Even if you are single, with no children, or family, you still have an extended family, of neighbors, co-workers, or associates, etc.

As you can see, this self-Inventory process is no easy task, but it is vital to the essence of your being. Self-inventory is often not a pleasurable process. You may find out some things about yourself along the way that you don't particularly like, but at least you will be aware of them. I will always remember the third day of class in which I was taking a self development seminar with Landmark Education, where I had a homework assignment where I had to share some things with a family member. I asked my sister Vivian to tell me something about myself that I may not have been aware of, but that I needed to know.

Those words she used to describe me still ring in my ears today. She told me bluntly, but in a sweet caring way, "You are arrogant". I was in total shock. The words that followed were even more shocking. She added, "I thought you knew. Yes, you are arrogant; you just do it in such a charming way."

Naturally, I was defensive about it at first, but then she pointed out a few incidents, and she was right. She not only told me, but she showed me the truth. And I thought I was such a sweet person. I did say that this was not an easy process, but it is a necessary one.

We need to examine where we are in life, how we got there, and how to get to the next phase in life. So take the time, and make a difference in the quality of the life you live. You can do it now, or you can wait. The choice is yours. After all, this is your inventory. There is no shelf life, expiration date, just the time you invest.

We usually don't see ourselves as other people do. That's why it is essential that we take the time to get to know ourselves. We must take personal inventory of our strengths and weaknesses to determine what we are best suited to do in life. This next young lady, took the same skills she applied in her position as Marketing Director for V103 radio station, and started her own business. She's the lady behind the scenes who made Chicago, the steppers capital.

Merry Green
Merry Green Productions
Expo For Today's Black Woman
V103 Stepper's Set

We all have choices in life. Sometimes we make choices that benefit us, and sometimes we don't. Merry Green, former Marketing & Promotions Director of V103 radio station, was one of those people who felt she had no choice in life, but to become the person she is today. Ms. Green says, "I never had a choice. Plain and simple."

A teen mother at the age of 17, pregnant again at 18, she had two sons to provide for by the age of 19 years old. Merry did not want her future life to be like her then situation, a single mother, raising two sons with a questionable future. Even before her pregnancy, she always knew that she w anted to be somebody, and she didn't let her situation stop her.

Her career as an entrepreneur, was a natural progression for her. Self motivated, hard working, and getting the job done, was what she was known for. Her reputation preceded her. A native of Rochester, New York, she moved there at the age of ten with her parents from Nashville, Tennessee. She was Assistant Producer at a local television station. She moved to Chicago and joined NBC as Producer of Public Affairs Specials.

It was there that she gained a reputation for her expertise in creating ideas to help corporate clients expose their products to the African American community through promotions and on air commercials. She always kept her word, doing as she'd promised.

Ms. Green says, "What prompted the idea to go into business for myself, was a culmination of experiences. A casual conversation with then General Sales Manager Chris Wilson at V103, (now at the Loop) encouraged me to take the steppers project, as well as other projects I had, and do my own thing."

She fondly remembers after three years, the project had really outgrown the space they were in at the radio station. She adds, "The phone lines were always overflowing with calls, and it was just too much responsibility to handle in addition to my position as Marketing and Promotions Director. I always wanted to do something positive in the community, provide education and information that would focus on women and their families, and do it better than it had ever been done before."

As Marketing Director, she knew her sponsors target market were African American Women. She wanted to do more than the listener parties and promotions and concerts, but to actually do something good that would benefit the family as a whole. She had envisioned something larger than she'd ever dreamed. She saw a need, and filled it. Plain and simple. She had no choice but to be the best at what she does. Her sixth year as promoter of the Expo for Today's Black Woman is proof. With attendance over 750,000 men, women, and children, she's taken the expo on the road to several other cities including Orlando, Florida.

You can expect to see and hear more about this amazing young lady. She expected the best, because she gave and continues to give her best.

Let Ms. Green be a shining example of what can happen when you take the time to look within. Merry did it, and so can you. Don't worry about what resources you don't have. Work with what you already have. Remember, when you worry, you do yourself a serious injustice. This insert is taken from my daily MMM (MasterMinding Messages) Free to all. Simply email me at: Zelda@zeldaspeaks.com for FREE subscription.

Tuesday January 12

W.O.R.R.I. (WORRY)

WASTED
OPPORTUNITY TO
RELEASE &
RESTRUCTURE (YOUR)
IMAGINATION

Sometimes we use our abuse our imagination without really thinking about it. Why worry? It only brings into our experience of what we really want in life. Dr. Winston Johnson says, "Worry is the interest you pay on things yet to come."

To overcome it, set aside a particular time of the day, to do nothing but worry. That's right, schedule in some time in your daily planner, and keep that appointment with yourself. During that time, focus on what you are afraid of happening, and watch what happens.

Now if you really want to be effective, use that time to focus on what you really want. Then watch what happens. Notice the difference. Don't worry! Be Happy!

Chapter 6

Obstacles

"It Works If You Work It!"
-Rev. Dr. Johnnie Coleman
Founder and Minister
Christ Universal Temple
Universal Foundation For Better Living
Author of ***Open Your Mind and be Healed***

From the moment you awaken in the morning, until you fall asleep at night, life is full of obstacles, or daily challenges. As author/speaker Willie Jolley says, "It Only Takes A Minute." It is within this small time frame that we constantly make decisions based on our experiences and how we handle them. It not what happens to us in life, it's how we *react*, to what happens to us in life.

Once while I was sitting at a stop light, waiting for a red light to change, I was hit from behind by another driver. She jumped out of the car, and started screaming at me, yelling at the top of her voice, "Why did you jam your breaks?" Where on earth did you learn to drive?" At first I thought I was hearing things. This total stranger, who was obviously so upset about something else, that she didn't even see me sitting at the red-light, had the audacity to jump out of her car, and accuse me of causing an accident. Then, a thought came to me: "There's more to this than what meets the eye, and it has absolutely nothing to do with you.." When I didn't respond to her negatively as she did to me, I am sure she was more shocked than I was when she my car.

When she approached my car window, getting louder the closer she got, I looked her in the eyes and asked, "Are you okay?" It was like watching Saturday morning cartoons. She did a double take and looked at me funny, trying to figure out if I said, what she thought I said. She looked at her watch, then back at me. She then walked to the rear of my car, looking at the bumper, and then at her own broken headlights. Evidently she was fine, she wasn't hurt, just upset, and not about this accident that she had caused. "I'm okay " she said, "But my husband is going to kill me. I don't know what to do. Our insurance coverage is already on the verge of being canceled, and when I tell him about this accident, I know he's going to go through the roof." By this time, I could clearly see that this was a moment of truth. I could have joined in her pity party but instead Spirit allowed me to see this obstacle of being subjected to criticism and ridicule, as an opportunity to practice the principles that I had learned, and was sharing with my audiences.

This incident of overcoming the obstacle placed before me, was an opportunity for me to experience a new paradigm shift. There was one accident, but there were two different perceptions of what really happened. Her perception of what happened, and what really did occur. Regardless of what really happened, it's all in the perception. Something as minor as a traffic accident can ruin your whole day.

You can walk around with a bad attitude all day, thinking negatively about the situation, or you can try and learn a valuable lesson from the experience, and move on.

Many people allow circumstances to control their lives, and never learn anything from the experience, which is there to teach us something in the first place. We will continue to have these types of experiences until we learn the lessons, whatever they may be. An apparent *obstacle*, can be an *opportunity* in disguise. Once we can begin to see the obstacle for what it really is, it is at that point that we can begin to experience life on another level. It all depends on which paradigm in which we are operating from.

If we see the experience as a disaster, then that is what we will experience. More of the same types of experiences will continue to develop around us all day. It's a mindset. If you've made up in your mind that it going to be "one of those days", then this is exactly what you will continue to experience throughout the day. Remember the quote, "As a man thinketh, so is he?" Well, it definitely applies to this situation. One of the main reasons we continue to have the same obstacles repeated in our lives is because of our thinking, which has been conditioned.

It is only when we free ourselves from *conditioned* thinking, that we can begin to experience a new paradigm, and go with the flow. Once we make that mental shift, we will be able to see the obstacle for what it really is, an opportunity in disguise. What was your latest *opportunity*?

Only two weeks before going to print with this book, I

was always finding other things to do, instead of concentrating on finalizing the last details of completing this book. I was busy just running around, making public appearances, attending meetings, scheduling conferences, meeting with prospective clients to speak in South Africa, and finalizing other projects.

I was so busy honoring my commitments to everyone else, I forgot what my priorities were. Out of all the commitments I had made, I had broken the one, that was most important to me. The commitment to myself. To stop. To be still. To listen. I was not in tune with me. I was actually running from myself, by attending to all the other *stuff*, that I had committed to. This book was one of my top priorities, so why had I not brought it to completion? I spent most of the Christmas holiday season finishing up the last several chapters, and I was so proud of myself, to have kept that commitment to myself. By December 31st, I had completing writing this book, but I would not finalize the plans to get it to the printer.

Well, wouldn't you know? The Universe had a whole new plan in store for me. Just when I thought I was on a roll, I had an accident? This *accident* forced me to do what I had been warned by the Universe, to do earlier. It made me look at myself, and reorganize my priorities. The signs were there all the time, I simply chose to ignore them. The fact that my Toyota needed an alternator, and the Mercedes needed a brake job, was not enough to get my attention. It was only when I slipped and fell on some ice, right outside my apartment door, while doing my laundry one Sunday night, that I really got the message.

You see, I am the kind of person that does not take subtle hints. You cannot beat around the bush with me. You must come right out and tell me, point blank.

That's the best way to get my attention. Now that the Universe has gotten my attention, I can focus on my priorities. As stated in Chapter Four, Setting Priorities, it's crucial that we take the time to do that, otherwise, we wind up having to learn the lesson, the hard way. Don't wait until you're flat on your back to get the message. I have no choice but to be still, and listen, because the ligament I tore in my ankle will take some time to hear. Doctors say ligaments take twice as long as bones to heal. The specialist told me two to six weeks. Since I don't want to be off my feet for that long period of time, naturally I am opting for the two weeks.

It's only been a week now, and I can just begin to let my heel touch the floor, let alone put any pressure on it. This week has been an incredible one, because it has allowed me to have another paradigm shift. I knew the moment that I hit the ground that something was broke, because I heard something snap, but I also knew that the snap, was truly a blessing in disguise. That's exactly what any *problem, argument, confrontation, disagreement, illness, accident, incident, challenge*, *delayed opportunities, or obstacles* are. Blessings. Period.

Close your eyes for a moment, and think back to the last obstacle you experienced. Relive that experience, if possible. What was the first thought that entered your mind, when the experience first occurred? What were your thoughts half way through the experience? What were your final thoughts? Do you see a difference? Do you see how the situation that you viewed as detrimental to you, at some point, was actually something that happened for your own good? If not, try another situation. You have a multitude of experiences to choose from.

One of those experiences is bound to shed some light, that you once were not privy to. It is these kinds of experiences that make us grow, and step out of the security of what we think we know. We must always remember that the Universe works in accordance with us, whether we recognize it or not. The sun will rise, whether we arise with, or without it. The moon will shine at night, whether we go to sleep with it, or stay up all night. So don't stay up all night worrying about the possibilities of what might or might not happen, because of your present situation. As Dr. Winston Johnson, of Christ Universal Temple says, "Worry is the interest you pay on things yet to come".

So save yourself some interest, and allow the obstacle to teach you the lesson, that it has come to teach. Remember the saying, The teacher never comes before the student is ready?" Well, you must be ready, otherwise you would not be having the experience. What has your last obstacle come to teach you? The torn ligament in my ankle came to teach me, what I share with my audiences all the time, be still, and listen. The incident with my ankle is nothing compared to this young man, who is paralyzed from the waist down.

Melvin Mamon
Son of Mary Pearl Mamon
Sledge, Mississippi

Melvin Mamon is a young man in his thirties who was injured in a car accident, which left him partially paralyzed from the waist down. Naturally, as a result, he has to depend on others to take care of him. Since the death of his mother Pearl, he has to rely on the help of his sisters and brothers. It's truly a blessing that he comes from such a large family. When his sisters or brothers Maurice, Mary Deloris, Cherry, Buttercup, or David are not around, he can always rely on his big brother Robert, who lives in the next town, to go pick him up and take him for a ride.

Robert shared with me just how much energy Melvin has. Sometimes it's hard for him to keep up with his younger brother even though he is paralyzed from the waist down. Melvin refuses to let his condition stop him. He refuses to give in to the idea that there are certain things that he cannot do. He knows his limitations, but it doesn't stop him from trying. When he wants to go somewhere, and no one is available, he takes it upon himself to drive wherever he wants to go. He lifts himself out of his bed into his wheel chair, and seats himself in the drivers seat of his own car. He uses a stick to push the gas pedal and the break. He drives himself any and everywhere he wants to go. Talk about determination.

He's been doing this for the past five years. He gets around better than some people who have full use of their body limbs.

About a year ago, Melvin was admitted to the hospital for surgery. After only a few days of recovery, he tried to release himself. The doctors wanted to know why was he in such a hurry. He simply told his doctors that he was ready to go home. Period. The hospital made him feel like an invalid. At home, he could do for himself. The doctors had to explain to him that he needed to allow his body time to heal. His reply to the doctors was that he was already healed.

Despite the doctors prognosis, Melvin was released from the hospital two weeks earlier than his scheduled six week stay. Melvin is certainly an inspiration to me. He is more than inspiration. He is a shining example for others to see how they can overcome any physical limitations bestowed upon them. This experience has helped him realize that he is much more capable of doing more than anything he has ever done before. He is now more active in the community than ever before his accident, or should I say Divine Providence. God does have a way of pushing us more than we ever would push ourselves.

Whenever I think about what I can't do, or don't feel like doing, I think of Melvin. To many it would appear that because of his physical limitations, he would be depressed. He's anything but that. His spirits are so high, I believe that's why he's always surrounded by lots of people. People are always stopping by to see him, bringing him food, cakes and pies, or to just sit and talk. I am sure that many of those who visit him are amazed at his tenacity.

As W. Clement Stone once said, "There is really very little difference between people; it's called attitude; and it really makes a big difference. The big difference is whether it's positive or negative."

Remember, obstacles are what you see when you take your eyes off the prize. Melvin is clearly a demonstration that his attitude, determines his altitude. He will soar higher in a wheelchair, than many people will, who have the use of their legs. How high will you soar standing on two feet?

Chapter 7

Now!

There is a Universal Presence
that acts as though It were intelligent,
and we may assume that It is.

-Ernest Holmes
The Science of Mind

The nature of our being, is in the NOW moment. It is in this very moment, at this point in time, that we are living. Yesterday is history, tomorrow is a mystery, and today is all we really have, because we have no control over yesterday or tomorrow. We do have some control over the decisions that affect our lives. It is this moment that you have decided to read this book, this chapter, and this page, not necessarily in that order. However; it is without fail that the moment you made the decision to pick up this book, guided by Spirit, you made a decision, not to do something else. You decided to read.

So as it is with your purpose or your passion in life. What is it that keeps you from making the decision to pursue your passion, that which gives meaning to your life? And if you are pursuing your passion, what's stopping you from moving to the next level? Has your old way of thinking eased it's way back into your subconscious? (which is where we operate from.) Have those old thoughts gotten the best of you; and are they now holding you hostage?

My first day of on-air experience at a commercial radio station came as a result of one of the mid-day radio personalities calling in sick. I was sitting in the office of P.J. (Prehistoric Jammer) Willis, Program Director for the now defunct WJPC (Johnson Publishing Company). It was my third interview. He politely excused himself and answered a phone call from which he hung up with a sly smile on his face. P.J. scratched his head, thought for a moment, shoved his glasses back up on his nose, with a grin on his face I will never forget, asking me if I was ready to go on air.

I sat there with an even bigger grin on my face, completely surprised. "Do you mean, now? Right Now?", I asked, hoping that he really meant tomorrow, or next week sometime. I wasn't quite ready. I had practiced at school in the Radio Broadcasting studio for two years, waiting for this moment. Here was my opportunity, and here I sat, looking for a way out.

The counselors words echoed in my ears, "She'll never find a job in radio". It was those stinging words, that gave me the jolt I needed to force me out of my seat, as I followed P.J. into the studio to get a quick run through of how to operate the board. It was pretty much the same type of equipment that I had used at school. But the thought of a live audience (not my classmates) had me shaking in my boots. Despite the fact that the station had a low signal, they were number one in their market of what is now referred to as *old school.* Listeners clung to your every single word. Not a place for rookies. No time for mistakes. No time to practice. This was the real deal, Holyfield.

Armed with techniques I had learned in college, and all the little tricks of the trade I had picked up from my broadcast instructors, I walked into the studio with the spirit of Columbia behind me, hoping not to let them down, or make a fool of myself. It was do or die. Now or never. I would have chose never, but it wasn't available.

P.J. gave me the once over on the equipment, assured me that I could handle it, and left me in the studio to do my thing. My fingers ruffled through the program log, as I grabbed the commercial spots, the upcoming music, and prepared to open the microphone. I tried to cover both ears with the broken headphones, while trying to hear the music fade down, and opened up the mike to let Chicago hear the new kid on the block.

Zelda had finally arrived. I opened the microphone and let her rip. Pretending to be the voice of my favorite Radio Personality, Denise Jordan Walker, on WNUA 95.5, Smooth Jazz. I was so smooth, I even fooled myself. I almost fooled a few of our listeners, until a few people called in to ask where Gachelle Coffey was. Your Coffee in the morning, (her hook) was out sick. Those few seconds were the longest 60 seconds I had ever experienced. I could feel the tremor in my voice, and I am sure the listening audience heard it too. I was terrified that someone would call and say, "who is she, and get her off the air." But no one did.

I was glad to be alive again. I played the next few records, and tried it again. Did a backsell (told what was played) and then a front sell (the upcoming records) stated my name, with a smile in my voice and closed the microphone with a sigh of relief. It wasn't so bad after all. After the first hour or so, I was beginning to get the hang to it.

Once I had built up my confidence, I was on a roll, taking requests from the callers, finding the music, and starting the next song in record time. No dead air for me. Everything was fine until it was time to do the traffic report from Shadow Traffic. P.J. had left the office, and had not shown me which microphone to pod up, so I missed the first traffic report. Definitely a no-no. You don't miss paid commercial spots. As soon as the segment was over, I saw the hot-line light up.

The general manager, Charles Mootry, was calling, screaming in my ear. I wanted to hang up on him. I was already nervous enough. I was warned beforehand that you never hang up on anyone, especially management, unless you didn't want your job. I was also warned to never let the telephone ring more than three times before you answer it. It had rang well over three times. I was now even more afraid to answer it, but I had no choice. I knew what he was calling about. He was calling about the traffic report that I missed. The traffic report that brought in revenue to the station.

I knew that the traffic was being sponsored by a commercial advertiser, and that's how the station makes money, and pays my salary. So I knew I was in trouble. I answered the phone, pretending to be out of breath, like I had just come running from the ladies room to answer the phone. He was screaming at the top of his lungs, "What the hell happened to the traffic? Why was there no report? Who the hell are you? Where is Gachelle? Where is P.J.?" He was asking so many questions, too fast for me to even think. I waited until he stopped screaming and said in a slow, nervous voice, "P.J. stepped out to lunch, Gachelle Coffey is out sick, and I am filling in for her, and I didn't know how to bring up the traffic. I am so sorry." "Sorry? I hadn't seen sorry," he said, as he yelled at me to leave a message for P.J. to call him back immediately. Boy, what was beginning to be a fun experience, was turning out to be a disaster. Why did P.J. have to leave me all alone in the studio and the whole office? No one was there for me to talk to. What would I do?

Well, I survived that little ordeal, and it gave me the experience I have today. I have worked at that station and many others like it including WYCA, WNUA, V103's sister station, 106 JAMZ, on the Sunday Gospel Connection, 950 AM, and on Chicago's only motivational radio station, WYPA where I hosted a talk show, The Passion Principles. I currently host my own show Sunday mornings on Gospel Radio WGCI-AM 1390, Music of Love & Inspiration..

The point is that had I not taken advantage of that moment in time that was offered to me, chances are, I would not be writing this book, sharing those experiences with you. I had to take advantage of that particular moment in time. As Robin Williams said in the movie Dead Poets Society, and Black Panther Buddy Seal whose book is entitled the same, "Seize The Moment". That's exactly what I did. Nothing in life is guaranteed. We live day to day, with faith that tomorrow will come. Tomorrow may very well come, but the same opportunities may not come with it, that's why we have to grab the gusto while we can. No other company in America says it better than Nike, with the most pro-active word in the Universe. Now! So what are you waiting for?

It's been said, "There are two kinds of people in this world. People who wait for their good to happen to them, then there are those who make things happen." Which one are you?

Instead of waiting for something to happen, go out and make something happen. That's what Dee Daniels did, after being fired from 106 JAMZ, former sister station of V103.

Dee Daniels
D. Daniels & Associates
Chicago - Bloomington - Schaumburg - Indiana

Former News Anchor at WCHS in Virginia, jazz Radio Host at WBES, WKDC, and Assistant News Director at WVSR, Daniels didn't wait for change to happen, she made things happen. When she moved to Chicago, she began as producer of the Denise Jordan Walker Show at WNUA 95.5, Smooth Jazz, and Radio Personality in Chicago, at WJPC and WEJM-106 JAMZ.

Dee was inspired to try radio because news was beginning to get boring. "There was no fun in it, and I always had the idea of doing radio in the back of my mind. So when I moved to Chicago, with a fresh slate, I tried radio and fell in love with it." She landed a position at WNUA 95.5, as a producer for the Denise Jordan Walker Show, where we both worked at the same time.

It was at WNUA that we met each other and I knew then we would be friends. She moved on to WJPC, where I wound up only a week after she was hired. When management changed hands again, she stayed for a short while, and then moved on to pursue starting her own Public Relations firm. With a wealth of knowledge and good contacts in the music industry, business picked up and she opened her first office on Chicago's magnificent mile, where only the elite have office space. Busting at the seams with new clients and opportunities, she opened a second office in Bloomingdale, Illinois for her suburban clientele.

The music industry is not for the lighthearted or thin skinned. Daniels says, "This is a tough industry period. For women or men, but particularly on women, especially if you're a mother. My daughter is my first concern. I am most grateful that I have family that lives near by and can keep and eye on her. She is with me most of the time, and she is leaning the business along side me. The biggest challenge is handling the paperwork and phone calls during the day, then seeing to it that the artists needs are met once they arrive in town for an engagement. I have to have my assistant make sure that their hotel arrangements, radio interviews, and tailor appointments are all in order. Nothing ever flows so smooth that we get things done at a decent hour. This career is not for a morning person. Don't get into this business if you have a nine to five mentality. You won't survive."

For Daniels, her greatest obstacle was in making the decision as to whether I would get another job in radio, or break out on my own. It wasn't an easy decision. Luckily, I had a husband who was a cardiologist, who supported my decision. Still an uphill battle because of our schedules, but we somehow managed. Still it was a challenge because the more my business grew, the less time I spent at home."

Daniels advice for newcomers interested in this business, is to know who you are and your limitations. Don't say you can, and you can't. Start out early and learn as much as you can. Be humble; you never know who you'll need a favor from. When building relationships with people in power, try to eliminate the middle man, and go straight to the top, or to the gatekeeper. Don't let others work your deals for you. Dee says that being fired from her job was the best thing that happened to her. It allowed her the opportunity to do what she always wanted, be her own boss. She calls the shots now. Who's calling the shots in your life?

Chapter 8

Practicing The Principles

"Practice Makes Perfect.
No. Practice Makes Improvement"
-Les Brown, The Motivator
Author, Live Your Dreams
It Ain't Over 'Til I Win

In order to get good at anything, one must practice. There's a quote that says, "Practice makes perfect", but that's not necessarily true. What practice does, is allow you the opportunity to become better at what you do. In order to excel in anything, you must repeat the process, until it becomes second nature, unless you were born with the gift, and then you still need to nurture and develop your talent to retain optimum performance.

I've known since my early adult life that my voice was my talent, but I haven't always known how to use it effectively. The majority of jobs that I worked in were either as a switchboard operator or as a receptionist. My supervisors always told me that I had a nice voice, so I used it to my advantage. Eventually I became bored with it because I had mastered it. I knew it was time to move on to something else. I wasn't sure exactly what, but I did know that I did not want another job answering telephones. I needed to learn how to use my talent in a way that was more challenging, and that would make me more money.

It was through the process of going to school, taking classes and seminars, listening to audio and video cassettes, that I begin to develop a plan. This plan helped me find a way to not only to build a career as a Professional Speaker and Training Consultant, an international one at that. When I first began speaking, I had no idea that I would travel to the other side of the world and speak to anyone. Not once, but twice in the same year, only three months apart. If that is not God, I don't know what is.

I have to continue to perfect my presentations, both on the radio and while performing seminars and workshops, because I never know when an opportunity of such magnitude will come my way. I do want to be ready. You often hear of overnight success stories, which are not necessarily overnight. By the time you hear of a new celebrity, that person has probably been practicing their craft for years. It just didn't happen. It appeared to have happened overnight, because the general public just found out about it.

Actor, Jhoumoun, who played Cinque in the movie Amistad, was homeless, living on the streets of Paris before he was discovered. He had been studying drama and acting for years before he got that part. By practicing your craft, when nothing seems to becoming your way, you are preparing for your good to come. Some might say that you are wasting your time, but once you hit the limelight, those same people will say, "I knew you could do it all the time."

Nairobi Kenya, East Africa

All the practicing that I'd done over the last few years was preparing me for my first trip to the other side of the world, to the Motherland, Africa. This trip made me look within, and challenge myself, to do the things I needed to do to make this trip a success, in ways I just never imagined. I didn't realize at the time that, but I was practicing many of the principles outlined in this book. I was definitely practicing the principle of Obstacles, as they were popping up all over the place. I was doing whatever it took to make this trip possible. I knew this was something I could accomplish. Many tourists had gone there before me, so it was not like I was breaking new ground.

What was unrealistic of me at the time (in which I wasn't even aware of) was obtaining a speaking engagement in a foreign country, where I had no idea of what there protocol was. It was definitely unrealistic for me, but it wasn't impossible. In America it is standard business custom to return calls within a 24 hour period. That was not the case with the managers with whom I was trying to contact. Now that I look back in retrospect, they probably thought I was crazy. A woman, from America, coming to their continent, trying to secure work. How dare I? Who did I think I was? This was the type of business that only men could secure. Not anymore. But, then again, that's just the conditioned side of me thinking. On this Corporate Continent, women are very much in charge in some areas.

One lovely Manager, I will never forget her, was Grace.

When you first saw her, you knew she meant business. And if she was working with the man who was responsible for bringing me in to speak, you knew she had to be sharp. And she was. She looked very stern, but her demeanor was quite the opposite. After speaking with her for only a moment, I was made to feel very welcome.

Welcome was not the first reaction I received upon trying to establish myself there before arrival.. There was certain protocol that had to be followed. You just don't decide you want to go, and show up. There are some preliminaries. I had to first make the necessary steps to insure my travel there, let alone have a presentation upon arrival.. From the very beginning, there were unexpected daily challenges that I never even anticipated. The moment I made the discussion, is the moment the ball started rolling.

The moment I committed myself, by signing on the dotted line, I was in for the surprise of my life. In the very beginning, I was beginning to become a little frustrated while making the necessary calls to make this trip possible.

All the calls needed obtain the necessary credentials to leave the country, and travel to other countries while on the continent of Africa, made me wonder was this trip worth all the hassle I was going through. The first step was obtaining my passport, which is another story within itself.

The vaccinations required for travel was almost enough to make me sick, which was ironic, because they were designed to prevent sickness. The simple thought of getting six shots gave me flashbacks from my childhood. I didn't like them then, and just because I was all grown up now doesn't mean I like them any better. Besides, I had a choice. I had no choice as a child. I could take the shot, or leave it. I still had a choice then. Take the shot and go to Africa, where I longed to go since I was a kid, or not take the shot and wait for the postcards from my friends. The choice was clear. I would take the shots, and save them the trouble of sending me a postcard telling me how much fun they were having.

Besides, send postcards was one of my favorite things to do, I didn't want to miss that pleasure. The whole trip itself was to be pleasurable, and I didn't want to miss any of it. In retrospect, I understand that the pleasure was in the whole process of preparation, which was part of the journey, even including obtaining my visa. Purchasing travel insurance (which was mandatory) was an experience within itself.

For a fleeting moment, I thought about whether I would need that travel insurance as my cramped, bruised aching knees weathered the two hour long, bumpy ride through the roads of Kenya, on what resembled a dusty road, filled with dips large enough to drop a small foreign made car into, and have enough room to get out of comfortably. I shivered at the thought of what it was like for my ancestors before me, who endured pain to much more degree than any tourist could even imagine. As Americans, we consistently complain about our highways and city streets, and we should, considering the amount of taxes we pay , but at that moment in time and space, I would have given anyone the keys to everything I owned, rather than crossing miles of unprecedented dust.

I compared this ride to a train ride on CTA (Chicago Transit Authority) on a nonstop route, ignoring all stops, seated in the one seater across from the conductor, with no lights, nothing to hold on to with no idea of where you're going, , and no conductor to get you there, fast. That's where I felt like I was heading. Nowhere. Fast. Nothing was in sight for miles and miles, except trees, a few villagers walking in the blazing sun, carrying a basket on their head, or some large sack on their back. You'd see a strayed animal every now and then. Most animals travels in packs. I could easily understand why. This was not a place to be alone. Animal nor human.

You here all kinds of strange stories about how Americans go to foreign countries, become hostages, and you never hear from them again. I had no intentions of becoming that kind of statistic. I had already beaten the odds by not ending up on as a single black woman raising 2.5 illegitimate, children. No way was I going to included in the next batch of statistics of prisoner tourists? Besides, I was a tourist, a woman. I was not a diplomat. I had no title, or large sums of money, like our Kenyan sisters and brothers thought. Most of them assumed that all Americans had millions of dollars just like Michael Jordan and Oprah Winfrey.

Sure, I have the developing consciousness of these millionaires, but my pockets didn't reflect it as of yet. I lived as well as they did while I traveled, (well almost) but This was a serious investment for me to travel abroad, even if it was by credit cards. If we didn't show back up at our hotel by the end of the day, I am sure someone would come looking for us.

Besides, we were members of the International Black Summit. We were there to provide empowerment to an evolving country. We were there for the good of mankind. Surely we would be missed. But then again, our people have been known to sell us out for a few pounds. (Africans are still under British rule and they use pounds, Americans use dollars) Although our history is that of an honest people, corruption is deeply rooted in practically every culture. This continent was no different. The real difference I had to distinguish, was the illusion I was under, and reality. Part of the illusion was all the fears and thoughts of others that I had brought on this trip with me, that were laying quietly in the back of my mind, waiting for the right opportunity to appear.

Our conditioned thinking has us full of so much fear of the bad things that could happen to us, instead of all the possibilities of the good that could. The reality was that these were honest people. Our hosts, Mr. & Mrs. Gatuhi were gracious enough to personally drive us take us to places we would not have had the opportunity to visit, on the tourist route. That's reality. I was even introduced to a very wealthy farmer who proposed marriage to me. Strange customs. I didn't even know the man, and he wanted to marry me already. Of course I declined under the watchful eye of the first wife who was giving me the old evil eye.

We continued our journey traveling to only one or two tourist attractions the whole time we were there, and that was downtown to the shopping center, an experience I will cherish. It was there, squeezed between vendors who fought for me to spend money at their shop, that I learned the art of bargaining, an old African tradition. It was a learning experience for us as Americans, as well as the Afrikaans who ran the shops for the

Arab, and oriental owners. If you really want a tourist to shop freely, don't crowd them, urging them to buy, buy, buy. Let them have there space.

Space seemed to be a commodity as we continued our ride on the rough terrain. Seated between myself and my dearest friend and roommate Linda Shepard, a seasoned traveler, was Another member of the International Black Summit, whose hips were not quite as large as mine, but her legs were. I shared her pain every time she moved, because in every move she made, I too had to adjust my legs.

As I turned at the slightest sight of a recognizable African animal, for my camera to catch a glimpse of my memories to take back to the states to show our family and friends, a sharp pain ran up the side of my hip like a bolt of lightning. Every time I tried to get a shot of my favorite animal, the zebra, it seemed to notice. The best photo I could ever get was of their rear ends. I wonder if they were trying to tell me something. I'm sure they had heard the sounds of shutters clicking over and over again, and just plain tired of the noise. After all, I was violating their space, even if it was with a zoom lens, several hundred feet away.

Barefoot was the norm in this culture, despite the advance of modern technology. I loved to see the children running around shoeless, laughing, playing, without a care n the world. It made me feel so at home, like I was back down south on my aunt Edna's farm, picking peas in her garden, and catching butterflies in between. Even during the 12 -14 hour days of the International black summit conference, where by the middle of the day, many of our Kenyan brethren had removed their shoes, and we followed suit. It was like being at home with family. I really enjoyed that. But I didn't enjoy it enough to remove my shoes just now. Cramped my feet may have been, but not enough at that moment to let the dust settle from between my toes.

I was afraid that if I took them off, I probably wouldn't have been able to get them back on. Your feet do swell when you travel if there is poor circulation. The only thing was circulating at this point was the dust that trailed behind the comfortably 4 seated jeep that carried the five of us, and the never ending thoughts of when was this ride going to be over with. I didn't mean to be unappreciative, but between the numbness in my behind, and my sore knees and legs, I was ready to scream. I kept reminding myself, it would be over soon and it would be well worth the distance.

From the time we left Safari Park Hotel, I was in constant awe of everything and everyone I laid eyes on. When we finally stopped at a store in the middle of nowhere to get something to quench our dusty throats, I was once again somewhat disappointed at the lack of enthusiasm our Kenyan brethren displayed toward us. I am not quite sure what I was expecting, but it definitely wasn't what I received. I should have gotten over the fact that these people were not going to greet us, total strangers, like we were one of the family.

That harsh reality slapped me in the face upon arriving at Kenya's airport. We were greeted with great big suspicious eyes. This moment was no difference. The only difference in this setting was that there were less people, in a closer proximity. Maybe I could ask one of them a question, and get an honest answer. Since our hosts were native Kenyans, I felt at home enough to do so, the moment the opportunity presented itself.

As we climbed out of the dusty jeep, one by one, we took long lazy stretches, like the leopards we passed on the road miles back. As I stretched, I noticed some young men standing ding, leaning over the rail of the building that housed the small grocery store where we were headed. More young men emerged from wherever they were, including an elder leaning on a hand built walking stick, a stick that he had probably made himself, with his old withered, wise, and wrinkled hands. Hands of a man who had seen the changes of at least a century. With quiet eyes, he gently watched us, as we watched the crowd milling around us.

One young man eager to sell us his wears, made his way through the crowd. He offered us sandals he had made with his own bare hands, from discarded rubber tires. Tires that were no longer of any use to any automobile, but that could be salvaged and designed to flatter such flat feet as mine, and provide food for a family. Talk about taking lemons, and making lemonade!

This is a prime example of using your raw talent. This young man had serious vision. He saw a way to make something out of what the average person would see as nothing. He clearly knew that his hands were his talent, and his vision was his gift. To have that kind of foresight is nothing less than phenomenal. "Then again it isn't anything out of the ordinary. It isn't anything that we should be surprised about. Each individual on this universe possesses the same talent and abilities as this young man, but because we live in such a modern, convenient society, we allow our talents and abilities to idle, while we use the talents and abilities of others.

When we allow ourselves some quiet time and space to tap into our own greatness, we become aware of talents and abilities that we didn't even know we posses. I have known since I was a child that I loved to write, I just hated typing. Little did I know it was typing that would help me mold my career as a writer. Just as this young man had molded a pair of sandals from a recycled tire, so can we use the same raw talent we possess, once we take the time to go within and discover our own hidden talents. This young man clearly had talent, as I suspect many of those who surrounded us did.

Out from the store came a young lady, no more than seventeen, with her baby gently wrapped across her back. As she grumpled with the small bad she was carrying, I couldn't help but to notice the doe shaped eyes of her baby, who enjoying the ride. I stopped her to coo the baby, and say hello to . We exchanged smiles, as I asked our host Mr. Gatuhi to translate for us, telling her how adorable her baby boy was. He was simply adorable. His smooth, coal black skin glistened in the sun, as he watched us curiously with doe shaped eyes. I listened to the exchange of frittering tongues, and saw the smile of a proud mother ripple across her face. She nodded he head as if in giving thanks, and continued to let us ooh and ahh at her pride and joy.

Her girlfriend beckoned her to join them. 'She motioned to us hat she was leaving, and begin walking in their direction, as they seemingly .eagerly awaited to hear the details of our conversation. They crowed around her and begin to chat and giggle as young girls do, oblivious to the strangers she just spoke to.

Upon entering the store, the familiarity of our great ancestors surrounded me. Here I was, on the other side of the world, on a foreign continent, in a land where I was not even recognized as African, but as American. Yet I was feeling so completely at home. It was as if I was back in the United "States, in the heart of the South, at the Hatley's store in Crenshaw Mississippi, a place where everybody knew everybody, and all of their business too, Home, but not home. Close, but so far away.

The woman behind the counter greeted us with a cross continental smile. She looked like any mother might look. Warm, and welcoming, with so much love you just wanted to hug her. She looked like she'd give you the shirt off her back, or in this case, the long pieces of fabric that swayed back and forth on the clothes line inside the store, that displayed her goods for sale. Only you'd have to purchase this material, after all, she was in business to make money, not give it away. Our host ordered a round of pops for us all. I don't usually drink pops because of the high acid content, and the fact that it gives me zits, but when you're in what seemed like the desert Africa, a hundreds of miles away from a fruit juice, you do as the natives do. I gladly drank a nice cold chilled bottle of sprite.

As I quenched my thirst, I began to look around the walls

and noticed the photo of Mr. Moi, the president of Africa. His picture seemed to be in every place of business. I wondered why that was. So I asked. It made little sense to me, but then again, I was not African, or so I had been reminded. The more I thought about it, maybe I should be proud because in American, there has never been a Black President. So why not be proud enough to have a photo of your Black President, in your black country? It was not something that I should really have been concerned about at that time.

I was more concerned with getting a piece of African cloth to wrap around my waist like the young girls outside were wearing. We discussed back and forth about which piece of fabric was prettier than the other, and which would be wide enough for my hips, I wound up buying two piece of the same cloth, and Linda bought another similar fabric. We were both quite satisfied with our new purchase of fabric from the motherland, ready to move on to something else. As a serious tea drinker, I could couldn't leave the store without some genuine Kenyan tea, and some beautiful straw hats to take back home as gifts. We finished our drinks, and made our way to the front door, where a couple of village girls were standing there watching us.

I noticed how the young girl had her skirt wrapped around her waist, and thought it would be grand if I could get her to show me how to tie mine the same way. She appeared to have not understood me, so I asked our host to explain to her what I wanted, and she obliged. We laughed and giggled as little girls do, while she wrapped the fabric ever so careful around my waist.

Despite the difference in the language barrier, she knew fashion, and she knew how to wrap that fabric to make me appear to look several inches thinner.

Linda suggested I buy her a pop for her efforts. What a great ideal. I bought her and her girlfriend one. Anyone who can enhance my figure without surgery deserves something cool to drink. We sipped sodas together, laughing, while the hot African sun breathed down on us. I commented on her ability to be a fashion designer, and she laughed a little more. By this time, others were crowding around to see what the foreigners were up to and they joined us in smiles. It felt so good. I felt so at home. Home. At last. Home with my African cousins whom I had never met before. Who did not k now me, nor I them. One thing we had in common, was the color of our ancestors. "The Diaspora had separated us, but the fabric reunited us. Home. It never felt so good.

I watched in awe as a young man with a hole in his ear as large as a spool of thread, walked past us, into the store. As he came out, I stopped him to inquire about the unusual size hole in the middle of his ear. I'm sure he could tell by the expression on my face, that I had never in all my forty years seen anything like it. He was probably use to foreigners gawking at him, and asking silly questions. Anyone who knows me, knows that I am full of curiosity. My first question was why? My second question was why so large?

Needless to say, he didn't understand either one. He did not speak any English, despite the fact that many Kenyans speak the "Queens English" very well. Better than many Americans.

My host graciously intervened and translated my question. I watched his facial expression turn from that of a frown, to a huge Colgate smile. The perfect set of teeth. The kind you see while sitting in the dentist office. They say these are primitive people. I say these are wholesome people who eat wholesome foods, and their teeth reflect just that. No dingy teeth here. Only captivating, curvaceous, Lilly white, teeth, a photographers dream, and a dentist worst nightmare. My host explained that it was a ritual in their tribe, the Maisai Maisai. A ritual of manhood. After seeing the size of the hole in his ear, I could understand why. Only a true Maisai Man, or any other kind of man, endure this kind of pain, willingly.

And I thought we as women had physical challenges. Not having birthed any children into the world, I could only compare this to childbirth. I t had to be excruciatingly painful. He explained that his initiation was very painful, but his family and made the process bearable, with support, and all the medical attention he needed. He assured my, via my translator, that if necessary he could do it again, but not voluntarily. I applauded his bravery, and acknowledged how I admired his human physique and how he wore the ear ornament with such pride. He was even nice enough to allow me a photo opportunity with him. This was truly a Kodak moment. Every time I think of that encounter, I think about what I would have missed, had I not gone out of my way to get my passport, to experience this precious moment in time. A moment that I would not have had to share in my seminars and workshops, and with you. A moment that made a significant difference in my life. Not because I was there in Africa, and got to take a photograph with an original Maisai "Tribe Warrior, but because of the challenges that I had, that I did not allow to stop me.

The challenge of taking three shots in the same arm this week, and two weeks later getting three more shots in the same arm, was all behind me now.. Arms that barely had time to heal, but didn't want to miss out on the experience of visiting the Mother Country, Arms that were too tired to reach over the counter to pick up the outrageously over priced prescriptions, that were mandatory. Arms that were reluctant to swallow the medication prescribed. Arms that were beginning to get weary from all the stuff they had to encounter. All of that, which made this Kodak moment, reality.

The reality is, where do we draw the line? Where and why do we stop at something that looks like it might be a little bit out of our league, or beyond what we think we are capable of accomplishing. The reality is we continue to live our present, out of our past. We subconsciously convince ourselves of our what we are incapable, without even realizing it. We must train ourselves to begin the process of reorganizing our thinking.

One of the best ways to do that is to immerse ourselves in activities that promote just that. Reading, listening to audio cassettes, and attending seminars, and by all means practicing the principles given in this book., which give us insight on how to live life fully It is with practice that you begin to see changes in your life and conditions The principles are the tools, but they don't work alone. They must be used by you, the architect, the one who is responsible for designing your life. These principles should be used properly, and consistently. They must be imbedded in the subconscious mind. We operate daily from our subconscious, which is programmed information. So why not program your mind to think in a way that is suitable to you?

It is never too late to re-program the computer of your mind. (Remember chapter 2 on programming?) so that you can experience life from a new state of awareness and enjoyment. I often hear people complain how boring their lives are. This is one of the reasons why people live such ho-hum, boring lives. They are still operating, functioning from old thought patterns. There behavior patterns can't change until their thinking changes first. If it's one thing I hope you get from reading this book, it is this. Your thinking shapes your life. Period. Ancient scripture says it plain as day, "As a man thinketh, so is he."

What do you think is one of the major reasons why some people barely survive in life, and others excel? It's simple. They have a plan, a mission, a purpose, a passion for living life to the fullest. They have broken the mold of conditional thinking. Changing your thought patterns are not as bad as you may think. Change is often related to something painful, or having to give up something. Change can be whatever you want it to be. You decide. If you begin to see change as something new and exciting, chances are you will begin to experience life in a more positive way. You'll have insights on a regular basis.

My new friends in Kenya gave me new insight, on the word passion. I thought I was passionate about what I do, until I met, and witnessed many Kenyans living with very little of anything. Many of them exist on so little, it literally bogs the mind.

In comparison to people in the United States who live on a fixed income, whether it's retirement, social security, public aid, or unemployment compensation, Americans live like royalty. Queens, Kings, Princes, and Princesses alike. We have so much to be thankful for, and don't even realize it. We (Americans) need to visit other countries to realize just how fortunate we really are. We live in a country that is by far, an abundant materially, but not spiritually. It's our individual responsibility to tap into our purpose and passion, so that we can begin to experience life, from a abundance consciousness.

What's your passion? How can you develop them? This is where your mission begins. We can have all the tools we need to build a foundation, but we have got to begin to practice them. Let's begin with what matters the most. The answers may not come immediately, but if you write a little something, say a paragraph each day, something will surface. You have to be willing, (surrender) to allow your spirit to guide you. Are you ready? If so, let's flip the page and begin.

Purpose

It's not always apparent what your purpose is, so if you don't know what it is just yet, think back to what you loved to do as a child? It may not be the answer, but it could lead you into the direction of finding your life's purpose. Everything you do along the way, is part of the journey, so don't be dismayed if you don't discover your passion so easily.

Find a nice quiet spot, where you won't be disturbed. Put on some nice quiet music, (my favorites are gospel, inspirational, or instrumental.) Play something that will allow your creative juices to flow. You don't want to play anything that will disrupt your flow of thoughts.

Have you ever been thinking one thing, and wrote something all together different that what you were thinking? Get my drift? Many people don't like to write, and that's okay. Just because you don't like to write, doesn't mean that you can't write. Writing frees the mind. Writing, scribbling, journaling, and anything else you want to call it, is a form of expression. It allows the spirit within you to express itself. In the process of writing, you free, that which has been held within you, that is waiting to express itself. That's why writing is crucial to the growth process.

It's more than just writing things down. It's a spiritual experience. That's why sometimes, you will write something so awesome, and wonder where it came from. You might even say to yourself, "Did I write that?" Sure you did. The spirit within you wrote it. Probably wanted to write it a long time ago, but you weren't open to the idea of writing. But that's okay too, because nothing ever happens before its time. As the saying goes, "When the student is ready, the teacher will appear." So if you're ready to accept that which you have been blessed with, begin your journey here.

Complete the following:

As a child, I used to love

1.

2.

3.

4.

5.

(write the first thing that comes to mind, not matter how crazy it seems.)

As a child, I always wanted to:

1.

2.

3.

4.

5.

Are any of the things you wanted to do as a child, still alive in your life? It's never too late to do some of them. Which one will you start with first? (refer to your list above.)

.cceptance

What is it that I need to learn to accept?

(Always write the first thing that comes to mind, no matter how crazy)

In my personal life, I need to accept

1.

2.

3.

4.

In my professional life, I need to accept

1.

2.

3.

4.

In life period, I need to accept the fact that

1.

2.

3.

4.

5.

This is your chance to connect with the part of yourself that knows all the answers to any question you may have. You must sit still long enough to hear the answers, and be willing to work with them. If you feel resistent or uneasy during this process, do it anyway.

Surrender

I surrender (let go)

1.

2.

3.

4.

5.

Setting Priorities

My number one priority is

The *second* most important thing to me is

The *next* most important thing to me is

Inventory

What personal characteristics can I improve on?

1.

2.

3.

4.

5.

Obstacles

What am I currently facing a challenge in?

My personal life

The first thing I can do is

If that doesn't work, I can always

If A or B, doesn't get the job done, I can

My professional life

The first thing I can do is

If that doesn't work, I can always

If A or B, doesn't get the job done, I can

What can I do to over come that challenge?

The first thing I can do is

If that doesn't work, I can always

If A or B, doesn't get the job done, I can

Now!

I must work with what I have, right here, right now. I can't wait

until____

Right now, I do have

____

Right now, I can

____

Right now, I know

____

Right now, I feel

____

READ THESE AFFIRMATIONS ALOUD, DAILY.

Right now is the only time I have, because tomorrow is not promised.

So I use my time wisely. Today, right now I will

I realize that my time, and talent is precious.

I recognize that there is something very special, happening to me now.

- I do not resist the urge to do what spirit tells me to do.
- I am in tune with the divine plan that the Universe has in store for me.
- I accept my blessings now.
- All really is well in my world, especially when it appears not.

In order for these affirmations to be believable, it helps if you repeat them three times, so that they will be recorded into the subconscious of your mind. Remember, practice makes perfect? No. Practice makes improvement. So to get better at anything, we must practice. One day, it will be. Actually, it already is, we just have to realize it.

Do yourself a favor and get a recorder, and record your affirmations on audio cassette. Play the audio cassette before going to bed at night. Research has shown that this is much more productive than falling asleep with the television on.

Bob Starshak says, "The third eye has 20/20." So learn to use your inner vision, instead of relying on your physical sight. Learning to use the third eye, is a challenge, but it can be accomplished.

Write your own affirmations on the next page.

Affirmations:
Tools for changing your consciousness. Powerful words build powerful beings. Empower yourself.

1.

2.

3.

4.

5.

6.

7.

8.

9.

10.

Chapter 9

The Plan

"To everything there is a season,
and a time to every purpose under
the heaven. A time to..."
-Ecclesiastics 3:1

The fact that you've read this far is a good indication that you're on target. You have greater works in you to accomplish. To accomplish those greater works, you need a plan. It's been said time and time again, in a hundred different ways, "If you don't know where you're going, any road will take you there.", "Where there is no vision, man will perish.", "If you fail to plan, you plan to fail." Planning for your future is essential. There is no such thing as security. True security lies within the essence of your own being. Once you realize that *you* control your own destiny, life will take on a whole new meaning for you. You won't wait for your ship to roll in; you will actively participate in designing that ship. You will be the primary architect of the kind of life you want to experience

You won't take chances on winning the lottery, which is about one in 25 million. Why bet on something when the odds are stacked so high against you? The money spent on lottery tickets, over a period of time could very well be invested in money market funds, or some other type of financial investment, that offers greater dividends after so many years.

Let this year, be your year of doing whatever is necessary (as long as it's legal) to begin the process of making the right decisions on how you want to live the rest of your life. A good way to do that is to take some quiet time out of your schedule, and make an appointment with yourself. Yes, that's right! Schedule some time in your Franklin Planner, your Time Keeper, or on just plain writing paper.

Mark on your calendar, the same time, (if possible) every week, to go over your priorities. Whatever is most important to you, in each area of your life. It's important to include your personal and family life because there needs to be a balance. You've heard the saying a thousand times I'm sure. "All work and no play, makes you a dull person." We need to be rounded. We have a tendency to pay more attention to certain areas of our lives than other areas. In order to create that balance, take the time to look at all the other areas of your life as well. (see Chapter 5, Inventory) It's not as important what you write it on, it's that you do write it down. So, go on and whip out that pen, pencil, keyboard, stylus or whatever. Make that move right now. You may choose these or other areas of your life that you deem important but the following is a format that I have used to assess and shape my priorities.

Spirit

How can I improve the quality of my life by tapping into my own inner wisdom, the part of me that has all the answers to all my questions? Here are a few suggestions:

Spend some quiet time alone first thing in the morning. Find a quiet spot where you won't be disturbed and simply close your eyes.

Practice a deep breathing routine that will allow you to listen to that inner voice. Simply, inhale and exhale through your nostrils, taking long deep breaths, focusing on your belly button. Try deep breathing for at least for a few minutes to still the mind, asking the Universe for direction. Read something on spirituality that will empower you. Read a variety of things, there's so much to choose from. I read from The Bible, Science of Mind Magazine, Creative Thought, Science of Mind book, the Daily Word, Acts of Faith, Pearls of Wisdom, Sister Feel Good, and my all time favorite, Iyanla Vanzant's, "One Day My Soul Just Opened Up." Whatever you are comfortable with, read it. There is so much negativity in the world, it's essential to arm yourself with tools that provide you with peace of mind before you begin your work day. Spend the first waking part of your day with the one who matters the most, YOU!

Don't wait until you're sick to take time out for yourself. Do it while you're healthy. The Universe will assist you. Ever wonder why you keep having the same health challenges? Keep getting sick? Listen to that inner voice, it's trying to tell you something. *Practice The Presence.*

Physical

As we get older, we have a tendency to be less active. It's vital to maintain optimum health. Do whatever it takes for you to cleanse your body on a daily basis. Do something to sweat daily. Walk at least a mile a day. It keeps the heart strong, and provides better circulation. If you can, get to the gym and workout. The body is designed to be physical. You've heard it before about the non-use of our limbs. "If you don't use'em, you might lose'em." A lot of surgery and removal of our limbs could be avoided simply be exercising. I don't particularly like it, but I do enjoy the benefits from it. It makes you feel good. There's nothing like feeling the adrenaline flowing, after a good work out. I guess that's why it's sometime referred to as a *natural high*. The body has its natural endorphins that produce this euphoria like state of mind, that makes you feel so good. It's unlike any other feeling you've ever had.

We all want to feel good, that's why we sometimes resort to using other stimulants, like food, drugs, alcohol, gambling, sex, etc. These *artificial* stimulants produce temporary highs, and they cost you dearly in the long haul. Sometimes the benefits don't outweigh the costs. Natural stimulants come from within, and they don't cost you anything, except a little of your time, and a little sweat equity. Spend a half hour or so in the gym or walking now, so you don't have to spend time at the doctors office or in the hospital in the future.

Anyone who knows me personally, knows that exercise is not one of my favorite things to do. So I compensate an hour long at the gym, (sometimes) by roller-skating.

Now roller-skating looks easy, but trust me, when you're out there on the floor, working up a sweat, it's not always easy, especially when you get tired around the fifth or six record. Skating to your favorite music makes it all the better. I occasionally can get in a request from the DJ, so I can really get my *groove on*.

When I don't make it to the roller rink, I practice walking 30-45 minutes daily on a treadmill. Sounds like a planned physical routine to me. What can you do physically, that will get your body moving? Skating, bike riding, walking, running, tennis, swimming, any kind of base, volley, foot, basket, or any kind of other ball you can possibly think of? Whatever activity you choose, be sure it's something you like to do, otherwise you probably won't do it. The only prerequisite for your physical activity is this. **IT MUST BE SOMETHING YOU LIKE TO DO. IT MUST BE FUN!** How much time will you spend improving the quality of your physical health this week? Write it down. Keep those health appointments. The body will be there when you need it most? Remember the last time you got sick?

Family

The media reminds us every single day of how we are in the midst of a crisis in our families. The latest term used is *dysfunctional families*. Whatever term is used to describe us, it's never too late to make a conscious effort to make relationships better, in the lives of the people we care about the most. I am well aware that there some family members that we don't care to acknowledge. Those relationships require a healing. Simply work on the ones you can, by trying to be more understanding and patient. Everyone doesn't want the same thing. It's up to the individual to do his or her part. Ask yourself the question, "What can I do, to be a better member of this family? Whatever answer you come up with, practice doing just that. Sometimes, simply listening, can open up a line of communication, where there was previously none.

A good book to read on families is Stephen Covey's, "7 Habits of Highly Effective Families." John Bradshaw has an extensive video version where he talks about the family, that may be available at the library. Take the time to invest in your family. After all, you are one of the main components that make up the family. List at least two things you can do that will make a difference in the quality of your life, and the members of your family. Write it down, and refer to it weekly.

The first thing I can do is

____

The second thing I can do is

____

Career

How can I improve or excel in my career, that will also allow balance in the other areas of my life? Sometimes our work has a tendency to overshadow other areas of our lives, which we might neglect. Write down several things you can do immediately, that can make a difference.

The first thing I can do is

____

If that doesn't work, I can always

____

Can you schedule more time to spend with the family on weekends, and less time in the office? When it's all said and done, it's the family that matters. You can be replaced in the office. Look around. Half the managers in the workplace, are the same age as your children, or your nieces and nephews. Take a good, long look at yourself. When it's all said and done, on your death bed, I doubt if you'll say or think to yourself, you wished you'd spent more time at the office. You'll probably wish you'd spent more time enjoying life, having fun, being with family, or loved ones. Don't use time as an excuse. There is always enough time. Simply prioritize. Where there's a will, there's always a way to find the time to do whatever needs to be done.

Financial

Ask yourself this question. Why am I working? Write down the first answer that comes to mind.

I work because

1.

2.

3.

Ask yourself the question three different times, and see what answer you come up with. We all work for different reasons. Some work just to have something to do, but most people work because they have to. If we want to provide for ourselves, the necessary essentials in life, we need to have a source of income. A certain portion of our years are spent earning income, but just how much do we keep. A good portion of people spend as much as they make. It's not how much we make anymore, it's how much we keep. If all that we make is spent before we get it, what good does it really do to make it at all? What are the long term benefits? What are we really working for? Just to consume more material possessions? Is that what the essences of life, and living, is truly all about?

Ask yourself another question? Why do I pay everyone else, before I pay myself? Make a special effort to write a check out to yourself first, before you pay any bills. A good number to begin with is ten percent. Put that in a savings, IRA, money market account, or some kind of interest bearing account, where you can't touch it. The next ten percent should be a tithe to where ever you receive your spiritual fulfillment from, your church, place of worship, etc. Many people are so wary of tithing to the church, so for those who have that complaint, tithe somewhere else. There's always a need in the community. If you're at the grocery store, and see someone short of money, tell the cashier to add it on to your bill. Give money to a homeless person. It's not up to us to judge how they became homeless. That is not what this is about. Start a college tuition fund for a child in your neighborhood. There are all sorts of ways. You're pretty clever. I am sure you can think of many more. Get creative.

The last ten percent should be put in an investment of some kind. So, now that you're operating on 70 percent of your total salary. Sound impossible? It did to me at first, but it does work. The only way to find out, is to try it. Watch the difference it will make over a period of time.

Write down exactly what you will do with the first 30 per cent of your income.

The first 10 % I will pay myself $_____ per week/BI weekly at the end of 12 months, I will have saved $_________________

The second 10%, I will tithe to _________________________ because I know, as freely as I give, so shall I receive abundantly. the Universe always rewards me threefold. (and it does not always come in the form of money.) It can come in many ways: time, resources, discounts, etc. I expect, the unexpected gifts that the Universe is waiting to bless me with.

The third 10%, I will invest in _________________________

at the end of 1 year I will have accumulated $_______
in **five** years, I will have accumulated $____________
in **ten** years, I will have $_______________
in **twenty** years, I will have $$$$$$$$$$$__________

Over a period of 5-20 years, you will have accumulated a small fortune, and it began with only a few dollars a month. That's the stuff real millionaires are made from. People who are serious about their long term finical welfare, invest in themselves now. See you at the bank.

Educational

It's never too late to learn. Ask yourself the question, "What can I do to learn more, that will improve the quality of my life, and those that mean the most to me? Life itself, its the best teacher. Experience will teach us things that we will never learn from books, but that doesn't mean that we should stop reading just because we've graduated from an institution of higher learning. We can always learn new and exciting things simply by going to the library, checking out a book in which we have absolutely no interest in. Going to seminars, workshops listening to audio cassettes, watching educational programming, going on field trips with the kids, etc. There are all sorts of ways to continue to educate yourself, without having a formal structured classroom setting. This sometimes scares people away, especially if you haven't been in a classroom in 10 or 20 years. I had an eight year lapse between completing degrees. Most of the students were in their teens, while I was in my thirties, but that didn't stop me. I know you're not letting that stop you. So what's your plan?

Social

I have come to a point in my life where socializing is not a priority. Most of the type of socializing I do is work related, so I have the opportunity to enjoy myself, and make new contacts simultaneously. It is important to remember, that everything does not evolve around the work environment. Sometimes it's healthy to make a date or have a night out with the girls or the fellows. Balance is essential. That doesn't mean you have to feel your calendar, or be at the *right* parties, but do take the time and enjoy your free time, if only going to the theater, a movie or play, or meeting someone for coffee or tea at a book club. Sometimes the best company is the quiet kind. A good book is sometimes all the company you need. What's your social calendar looking like? How will you divide your time *with* yourself.

To further encourage you to continue working on your plan when you feel like giving up, read the final chapter. This chapter includes people just like you and I who continue to make a difference in the quality of life for themselves, and their community. In the words of William Becton, "Be Encouraged". Have enough courage to make your own plan, so that no one else will have control over your own destiny.

Using your background as a reason why you haven't done anything constructive with your life, is the poorest of poor excuses. Many of our parents, and their parents, were raised with little of anything. What is amazing is how they took the little they had, and did so much more than many who sit around today doing nothing. What's even worst is that they complain about what they don't have. Success is an attitude. This next young man proves that you can do anything in this life, if you make the decision that you *can* do it and have a plan.

Dr. Winston Johnson
Principal-Washington Elementary School
Assistant Director Johnnie Coleman Institute

Growing up on 47th street being exposed to a lot of people whom we now refer to as dysfunctional, was common place. People who were drug addicts, drug dealers, or alcoholics usually ended up in one of three places. In jail, drug addicted, or dead. Not much has changed. There is an exception to every rule. Dr. Winston Johnson, is that exception.

As a young boy, Dr. Johnson was devastated when his father left the family when he was only 6 years old. After his father left, his mom took him and his two brothers to live nearby with their grandmother. It was his grandmother who really built the foundation on which he lives. It was a tremendous learning experience for him. His father's departure left him in shock. He really took it personal. He couldn't figure what he had done that was so bad, that would make his father want to leave. It also left him with a pain so deep, it had a significant impact on his self esteem. He failed not once, but twice in elementary school. Once in 4th grade, and again in the 5th. Can you imagine how that makes a child feel?

With that in mind, you would think that a child of his seemingly misfortune was doomed for failure. Not this child. After two failures in elementary school, his future for high school was looking bleak. His journey getting into high school was no easy task. He wanted to attend Tilden Technical High School, but his test scores were too low. He scored two grades below the grade level required for admission.

Experiences with fear and failure, coming out of an environment where there weren't really a lot of successful role models, he had to overcome the notion that ultimately much of what he observed that was happening to everyone else was also going to happen to him. Getting past the challenges, and not having a strong male role model in the form of a father was something that he had to get past. Dr. Johnson says, "In retrospect, I think I overcame it by learning that if you persist and insist, then life ultimately opens up to you. When I got to Tilden Technical High School, I literally begged the counselor, whom I will never forget, Ms. Eloise Fitzgerald to allow me to get into that school. I asked her what was it that I needed to do to get in? Her response was that I needed an 8.0 reading score to be accepted. I told her that my score was not that high, and she told me point blank, that I would not be accepted." But that didn't stop him. He continued to beg.

Dr. Johnson thinks for a moment before saying, "That was really an example of *Ask and it shall be given, seek and ye shall find, knock and the doors shall be opened to you.* Some of us ask, and don't ask anymore. Sometimes you just have to keep on asking. Some of us seek and we don't get the response that we want, and we stop seeking. Sometimes you gotta keep seeking. Sometimes you knock, and simply because you don't get an answer you stop knocking. Sometimes you gotta knock loud enough for people to hear you. So I kept asking and seeking. I really didn't know what I was doing at that time, but I wanted in. So I kept knocking and ultimately she said they would let me in on probation."

That was the turning point in his life because in his first year of high school his reading score went from 6.0 to a whopping 8.6, over the required reading level. That was his first experience of success, in which he teaches young people all the time. With confidence Dr. Johnson says, "*There is nothing that succeeds like success. Success builds self respect, and self respect builds up confidence, and when you build up confidence, it improves your performance. When your performance improves, that literally is the definition of success. The cycle starts all over again. Success then becomes it own form of motivation.*"

As a student at Tilden Technical High School, he was a pretty good student in his sophomore through senior years, but he didn't start out that way. It took him a little while to catch on to what high school was really all about. As a result of his good grades his teachers used him to tutor students who were having difficulties particularly in chemistry, in which he excelled. The day before the college representatives came out to talk to students about attending colleges and universities, representatives from the Chicago Teachers College were in the library of his school. His chemistry teacher, Ms. Rita Dunn, suggested that he talk to the representatives from the teachers college. She told him that he had a talent for teaching, and he might find it to be a good career option.

He went downstairs the next day and spoke to the representative, and from that conversation began his career as a teacher, that eventually led to Principleship. Dr. Johnson adds, " It shows just how easy it is to be moved in either direction. Just as a teacher could have suggested law or medicine, she could have told him to forget about college. Malcolm X was told to gear his skills toward custodial work because he could never be a lawyer. Just a word from someone whom you have a tremendous amount of respect, could send you in an entirely different direction."

As a result of getting past that hurdle, he went on to graduate number seven in his class, becoming a member of the National Honor Society. He went on to get a bachelor's degree from Chicago's Teachers College, and then later obtained not one, but *two* Masters Degrees, and a Ph.D. This is really demonstrative that if you hang in there, ultimately you will succeed. Nothing really stops you, but you. With a smile in his voice Dr. Johnson says, "The best definition of losing in life, is not failing , but quitting. You lose when you quit. Although my IQ was average, I learned that IQ doesn't mean anything unless the letters I-Q means, *I Quit.*"

Dr. Johnson shares his life experience with others when they began the song and dance of how they never had a father, or that they come from *the hood.* (neighborhood) It's the same place he came from, and he's taken his life and made something of it. They can do the same. With laughter in his voice he says, "I tell people all the time, that if they came into my neighborhood on Saturday after midnight, your chances of being robbed was 150%. *Guaranteed.*" This was during the latter part of the 40's and early 50's. Those experiences have really afforded him the opportunity to work with the young people. When they go to him walking the walk, and talking the talk, it's no stranger to him. A lot of the things he see them going though, it's something he experienced directly or indirectly coming up on 47th street as a young boy.

He quickly adds, "Although I was around a lot of drug addicts, they would always tell me, don't end up like me. I remember once waiting for a bus on my way to school, a brother who was addicted to drugs who looked like he had just a bad night walked up to me. He said to me, You see me? Look at me.

Don't you *ever* touch this stuff. I don't ever want to see you coming near this stuff. You stay in school, and don't ever end up like me" Unlike what we see in many instances today, a lot of the adults, not all but many of them, encourage children to become involved in those negative patterns of behavior. Luckily my experience was that when you came in contact with somebody who had experienced some serious problems with drugs or alcohol, they would use their own demise as an example of what you should never, ever become."

Dr. Johnson's *coming*, has had it's challenges. It took him over *10 years* to get his Ph.D. (Yes, there is still hope for us.) He admits that on a very subconscious level, he doubted if he could really do it. When he first started talking to the directors of the program and getting his paperwork in order, they told him everything was in place. He admits, "I would get myself involved in doing other things, which I think was a form of self sabotage. I'd stop working on my doctorate to do workshops, then go and take some classes on unrelated subjects. I would make a commitment to speak somewhere, which would require me to spend hours of preparation, taking up even more of my time. I would always justify doing it because it was something that I was supposed to be doing, because I was filling a need in the community. Then I would neglect my own doctoral work and when I would try to get started again, it would be so difficult for me because I would sometimes simply forget what it was that I was doing."

Puzzled and confused from his own writing, when he would try to pick up where he'd left off, Dr. Johnson would have to ask himself, " What did that particular notation mean? What was I trying to say in this particular interview? As I went through the program it was clear to me that I was sabotaging myself, trying to give myself a legitimate reason for failure. It wasn't until I was able to come face to face with that reality, that I could move forward." With a chuckle he adds, "You can't fix, what you won't face. I had to face that fact that I was setting myself up for failure. I decided that I was playing a game with myself and nobody was playing it, but me. So when anybody would come and ask me why didn't I finish my doctorate, I could say, well you know I was so busy doing other things like workshops, speaking engagements, etc. I could always justify it because I had engineered a path of going in another direction. Once I came to closure with that, I moved on. I was the one who was creating my own obstacles. Once I got myself out of the way, I finished my work."

Despite the decade of indecision, Dr. Johnson is a man who has faced difficulties, and has committed himself to share those seemingly failures with those who need it most. He has founded a male mentoring program to address the needs of young men, who are now experiencing major challenges. He knows that the only major obstacle you face in life, is really yourself. Once you decide that you are the only one that prevents you from doing what you need to do, you can begin to move yourself out of your own way, and begin to take steps in the direction of completing whatever you have chosen to do. It is possible. He is a living, walking, talking, fire breathing spirit cleverly disguised as a man, spreading the truth. He is an exemplary example. When Dr. Johnson speaks, even E.F. Hutton stops to listen.

A man of modest means, Dr. Johnson says, "One of the things I learned growing up on 47th street surrounded by drugs, that I think saved me, was that I chose a role model who was a

Baptist preacher. I was surrounded by addicts, drug dealers and pimps, but the person I chose was Rev. C. J. Rogers. Rev. Rogers was the pastor of Mt. Eagle Baptist Church on 46th and St. Lawrence. I'll never forget going to his church every Sunday. I would watch him tirelessly, noticing his every move . I even tried to emulate his walk. He had one leg shorter than the other, and I used to walk around the house trying to imitate him. My grandmother would say, Fool, are you out of your mind? This man has one leg shorter than the other, and you got two good legs, and you trying to walk like him."

You could see the smile come across his face as he spoke of this man of the cloth. He was just that much into him. He liked the way he dressed, he even liked the car he drove, which was a big, long blue Cadillac. The car Dr. Johnson drives today is a few years old, but it's the same color Rev. Rogers car was. Unbeknownst to Rev. Rogers, he was molding a life. He would become what would someday be a role model for children of a whole new era. He probably had know idea that his legacy would live on through Dr. Johnson.

As a little boy, Dr. Johnson remembers sitting in the balcony of the church, watching him preach, hanging on to his every word. So many of the young people were using pimps and pushers as their role models because they had items of conspicuous consumption, but not Rev. Rogers. This man was consumed by the word of God, and his actions spoke louder than any temporary high that any drug, could ever produce. Even as a child, Dr. Johnson's spirit knew that, and latched on to Rev. Rogers as if his breath depended on it.

His grandmother saw to it that his Sundays began at church, staying there until 2 o'clock in the afternoon. From there he would go to Rev. Louis Boddie's Greater Harvest Baptist Church on South State Street from three until four in the afternoon. He would leave there and go to Rev. Clay Evans church, which was at the time in a renovated garage on 46th and State Street. He would visit there from 4 until 5 in the evening. Finally he would leave Rev. Clay Evan's church, which is now on Princeton, go home for dinner and go back to Rev. Rogers church for the evening broadcast service. That service was from 6:30 until sometimes 9 or 10pm at night. It was that exposure to the religious and spiritual community that kept him out of harms way.

It was also to his advantage that he lived in close proximity to the church. After services were over, he would sit on his balcony and watch Rev. Rogers and his wife lock up the church. He would wave to him as he drove past his house. In the voice of a proud child whose father had just won an Olympic gold medal, Dr. Johnson beams with excitement remembering Rev. Rogers. He says, "I would watch that long, blue Cadillac until I could see no more." He paused for a moment, adding, "I doubt if he ever really knew how much I was into him except on one occasion when he and I were coming in the door at the same time. He asked me how I was doing. He shook my hand. That was our first physical contact, and it really kept me focused. His qualities, characteristics and attributes were all that I needed, and have sustained me until this point in my life."

Dr. Johnson's qualities, characteristics, and attributes are felt in the lives of those who listen. He tells everyone from his students, faculty, family, and the congregation of Christ Universal Temple, where Rev. Dr. Johnnie Coleman is Founder and Pastor, the simple truth. He says that truth is, "Whatever you chose to do in life, start with God. In all they ways acknowledge him and he will direct your path. Greater is he that is in you than he that is in the world. God's nature is absolute good. So when you start any journey with God, no matter how many obstacles you face, no matter how many battles you have to go through, you always turn out good.

Even more important is to believe in yourself, because it doesn't make sense to believe in God, if you don't believe in yourself. We are created in the image and after the likeness of God. That doesn't mean God in form, because God is spirit. You can't believe in God without believing in yourself. Know what you want to do in life. Ask God."

Dr. Johnson wants to be sure that students have an idea of what they want to do in life early on as possible. He found out what he needed to do by accident. A chemistry teacher told him the day before the college people came out, that he could probably be a teacher. That should have been formed and developed much sooner in life than his senior year in high school. With emotion he adds, "It should not have come as happenstance, just from a suggestion. Just as she suggested my doing what I am doing today, somebody else could have suggested that I do something quite different. I think you should take control of your life, because if you don't somebody else will. You take control by making a conscious decision to make a choice about the things that you're going to say *yes* to in your life. Once you decide what you're going to say *yes* to, you will say *no* to anything that is opposite. Last but not least, be too legit to quit. Never quit. You don't lose when you fail, you lose when you quit."

Quitting, blaming others, and procrastination are not characteristics of people who are living according to their purpose. Neither are they characteristics of your true self. If any of these false profits show up in your life as the drug dealers and alcoholics did in Dr. Johnson's life, change your direction and find a role model. It doesn't have to be a minister, just someone of high standards, whom you admire and respect. Begin to mold your life according to the divine plan that has already been established for you. Just as Dr. Johnson was watching Rev. Rogers, he was setting the pattern for this man's life. Someone is watching you. Whose life are you molding?

Chapter 10

Success Comes In All Sizes

"The challenges and obstacles you encounter in life, are the lessons that help you discover your inner resource of love, faith and strength."

-Susan Taylor,
Editor, Essence Magazine
Author-Lessons In Living

We often allow society to determine how successful we are. If we don't graduate from the right college, earn a certain amount of income, have office space on the right street, drive the right car, earn a certain amount of money, shop at the right stores, lunch with the big boys, marry a doctor or a lawyer, live in the right neighborhood, vacation at the right resorts, and God forbid, attend the right social events, than we are not successful.

We should define for ourselves what success means to us individually. What success means to one person, is not success to the next person. Success doesn't always refer to where we work, or how much money we make, but what we do with the life we have been given. Some people experience more success than others, and that in itself, is only a mere perception. It is that perception that filtrates our being.

The following stories all have elements of success which are included in them, but to what degree, is determined by the *individual,* not society.

Dr. Dennis Kimbro, Author
Think & Grow Rich: A Black Choice
What Makes The Great Great!
Daily Motivations for African American Success
Wisdom of The Ages

The security of a career and high salary in Corporate America can sometimes be more of a trap, than a safety net. Renown Speaker and Author of several of the hottest books on personal and professional development, Dr. Dennis Kimbro, is a testament to this truth. He left his position in Pharmaceutical Sales in Corporate America to pursue this endeavor, which actually started as part of his research for his thesis for his doctoral candidacy. Halfway through his dissertation, writing about wealth, poverty, and dependency in Third World Countries, Kimbro decided to change the focus and examine those issues closer to home, in the United States.

Working in Corporate America and touring the speaker circuit was taking it's toll. Kimbro was running out of sick, personal and vacation days. He couldn't continue to both work in sales, and go on tour promoting Think and Grow Rich, A Black Choice. Something had to go, so he made the choice to do what gave his life meaning. With a passion for making things happen, he put himself in the position to be mentored by some of America's greatest leaders in the area of personal and professional development, by the Napoleon Hill Foundation, W. Clement Stone, and Michael J. Ritt.

The challenges of following his dream were compounded by different factors. Time, relationships, and financial concerns were mounting throughout the process. Not spending enough time with his wife and three children was a major concern. His speaking engagements kept him away from home and family. There was never enough family time. In the beginning, not being able to provide for them on a college professor's salary, and withstand touring costs was another factor. Throughout the journey, he withstood the challenges, and despite the mounting debt, Kimbro never filed bankruptcy, like some other well known authors. He weathered that storm as he has many others.

Dr. Kimbro says, "The price of leadership is loneliness. Not everyone is a leader. You will stand alone. He adds that you cannot be concerned with what other people think, say or do. It's not worth it, and it takes up to much of your time and energy. He advises us all to:

1. Follow on that which you desire the most

2. Develop a Gratitude Attitude.

3. Dedicate yourself to lifelong learning.

4. Recognize strength grows out of struggle.

A husband, father, doctor, humanitarian, and fellow speaker who took time out of his touring schedule to assist me on my journey to writing my first book, Dr. Kimbro is a prime example of what really makes the great, great!

Dr. Margaret Burroughs
Founder, Emeritus - DuSable Museum
Commissioner - The Chicago Park District

Burroughs, a woman who's known for making things happen, founded the first African American Museum of color in 1961. It is and has always been her philosophy and belief that the purpose of life, that her purpose of being on this earth, is to leave a positive legacy for those who come after us.

Dr. Burroughs had insight even as a young teenager. She wrote in her 1933 high school year book, "I want to make the world more beautiful and better, just because I am in it." What a statement to have come from such a young mind. From the mouths of babes. Burroughs is a woman of substance that has not had any challenges that she could not handle. She simply states, "I have learned that perseverance is what counts. You start to do something, and you just stick with it until you succeed. You don't let anyone or anything deter you from reaching your goal.

There are always people around who will help you if you need them. *Bread cast upon the water comes back a thousand fold.* Dr. Burroughs is proof that if you keep pushing in the right direction, something will give. She leaves us with words I have often heard my grandmother say, "Believe in yourself. Believe in your goal. Work to achieve it with all your heart and soul. Keep your hand on the plow. Hold on."

Dr. Burroughs has seen and taken advantage of the many opportunities afforded her, that many people will never experience. No matter how few the opportunities are, what matters is what you do with the ones that do come your way. Are you taking advantage the experiences that life is offering you?

Anthony Morgan
Owner, Pro Star Promotions
Former Athlete
Chicago Bears and Greenbay Packers

Watching his mother struggling as a single parent, raising his brothers and sisters alone, was enough to inspire Anthony to grow up and do something positive with his life. Instead of joining a gang, he became athletic, and got involved in sports, which lead to a career in professional football.

After seven successful years in the NFL, an injury sidelined him, which was a blessing in disguise. Having always wanted to be his own boss, he decided to become an entrepreneur, catering to Corporate America, making promotional items for major corporations such as Kraft Foods, Anderson Consulting, and many local banks.

One of his greatest challenges was people who said that he couldn't do it, that it wasn't possible, because he was a Black man in White America.

He proved them all wrong. He didn't believe the myth that the White Man was going to hold him back. He looked within himself, and with the help of God, used the same discipline he developed in sports to propel him forward in the business world.

He shares his greatest lesson, saying, "I had to learn to listen to my inner voice, and follow my dreams, because people around me just didn't have the vision I had. So I had to disassociate myself from those people. If was to succeed, I had to fail first, learn from those mistakes, and move on. That's the way to learn about yourself and grow as a person. Anthony says,
"The best advice I could share with anyone is to know and believe in thyself first. If God gives you an opportunity, use it. *Write down your dreams and surround yourself with people who believe in you."*

It's a good thing Anthony believed in himself, otherwise, he would not be the successful businessman he is today. Many athletes don't take advantage of their resources before it's too late. Are you pursuing your goals daily, or sitting on the sidelines waiting?

A. J. Parker
Radio Personality

Inspired by her father, Chicago radio legend Al Benson started his career at WGES and WGRT, his daughter A .J. has taken radio by storm. As a child she was always right there at his side in his home studio.

Little A. J. learned to use her gift of gab, making her own way in the radio industry, not known for its kindness to women. Like father like daughter, her work speaks for itself. A.J.'s greatest gift is being able to touch peoples lives in a positive way. A. J. says, "It's my gift, and I give it freely to others." A. J's greatest challenge was when she made the decision to move away from Chicago to pursue a syndication career. It was especially hard to leave behind a very close family.

"My biggest obstacle is being a woman in this business and not being taken seriously. Positions as co-host are more acceptable than hosting a show alone, as if a woman is not capable of holding an audience, A. J. says." She finally adds, "I am not some push button giggle box." Listening to the response of her callers who simply l-o-v-e Ms. A. J., is evidence of that.

A.J. is continually mastering the art of balancing the demands of maintaining home and cultivating a career. Her work, though important, does not take priority over caring for her family. Nevertheless, plans for extending her family and having more children were put on hold. As a young woman who is still of childbearing age, she wonders whether she would have another child.

In making these choices, she has had to work 10 times harder on the job, and at home, 20 times harder. But the point of the matter is that she did it. She survived. You can too. A. J. speaks from her heart when she says, "If I can do it, so can anyone else. When one door closes, another opens."

Her advise to newcomers in this business is plain and simple. "Be strong, stay yourself, do not imitate anyone. Most of all stay grounded, because when you fall, the pain won't be as bad. STAY YOURSELF, DO NOT IMITATE, and I will say it again, this is the most important one, STAY GROUNDED, because, when you fall, the pain won't be as bad. You can get up, brush off those knees and keep moving on. There's also there's a myth, that in radio, you have to move out of town to succeed, don't believe it. Remember this, As a man thinketh, so is he."

Her career began in high school, and she moved on to work at station WVIP in Michigan. From there she went to WLNR, an all female radio station, then to WGCI AM and FM. She was wooed from WGCI to WJPC, which later transferred ownership, and was changed to WEJM, 106 JAMZ, (sister station of V103) where we both worked together for a short time. ABC NETWORKS in Dallas Texas made a syndication offer to A.J. She co-hosted a show with Doug Banks, which aired in over a hundred different markets. What is A. J.'s career choice now that she's back in Chicago? "Wherever God's path leads me, I'll gladly go." she affirms.

You can bet that wherever that trail leads, A. J. will undoubtedly leave her mark. She will touch souls, and made a difference in others lives, on the air, and off the air. It's a gift, and as long as she gives, she can't help but to get back. Its the law of karma, "As you give, so shall you receive." A word to the wise, Look out Chicago, A. J. Parker is back ! There is no stopping this Diva of the airwaves.

Lester Coleman
Coleman Development Corporation

Former substance abuse counselor, turned activist and Coordinator for CADRE,(Combating Alcohol and Drugs through Rehabilitation and Education) received inspiration while listening to a Sunday lesson sermon titled "Rest and Disposition," at Christ Universal Temple, by the one and only Rev. Dr. Johnnie Coleman. Rev. Coleman gave this advice saying, "You've got a Big God, so you might as well have some big dreams!"

Lester says that Les Brown was very influential in his life at that time, because he was doing two hour seminars on Saturday, and Johnnie did the sermon on Sunday. Now that's a "supersized combo" of real value. Lester says his biggest challenge was his supervisor at CADRE, whose sole purpose in life was to make him miserable. Coleman says, "I now know that he was angel in disguise, because it made me dig deep inside me to find, and bring out the best in me."

As a result of that relationship, he resigned from his $30,000 year job with perks, a company car, and has not looked back. He adds, "What's so fascinating about this relationship, it caused me to become an entrepreneur, and start my own business. I went into partnership with two other businessmen, who I had not known until nine months before I decided to go into business. My new business partners are close friends with my mentor, Dr. Winston Johnson, of Christ Universal Temple.

My biggest lesson is keep God first, in everything I do, think and say. Order my steps, divine order. I know that all things are possible, and we cannot judge by appearance. I have never ever had such peace of mind as I have now. The greatest advice I could give to anyone is to trust God. That's what I love so much about Christ Universal Temple, it teaches us practical tips on how to live prosperous.

We don't have to wait for some pie in the sky, God's graciousness is always with us, all we have to do is recognize it. I don't have bad days in my life, I have bad moments in a day." To quote the Rev. Timothy Wright of The Interdenominational Mass Choir says it best, Trouble Don't Last Always". Lester took the time to listen to what the challenge was saying to him. Are you willing to do the same? Remember, nothing in life is eternal. It's only temporary. Don't sweat the small stuff, because it's all small stuff.

Sylvia Taylor
Public Health Educator
Cook County Department of Corrections
Division Nine-Maximum Security

Sylvia Taylor, former nutritionist, now the Public Health Educator, Ms. Taylor has an extensive history of helping people improve the quality of their lives. She coordinated a variety of workshops, which covered career development and continuing education issues. Taylor also worked at University of Illinois Chicago, in the teen obstetrics department, where she able to incorporate the multitude of skills she lay claim to and that eventually led to her current position.

At the Department of Corrections, security is a bottom line concern and poses some difficulties for Ms. Taylor. When she's in the middle of teaching a class, or has someone in someone in her office for counseling, they can't stay over the allotted time because they have to return to their cells. She's learning to go with the flow, and continue the meeting or class at the next session. Advice she gives to newcomers is to try and help the inmates to become better people, and chances are you become a better person also.

Ms. Sylvia, as the inmates affectionately call her, called me after receiving a referral from my sister (correctional Officer Foster) to come and speak to her class. I thank Sylvia for the experience, because it has allowed me the opportunity to not only practice my craft but gave me free publicity too. I read an article on the Internet asking for speakers who had experience speaking to inmates.

I responded, and was asked to write an article on that experience. It has been solicited to be included in Tom Lagana's, of Wilmington Delaware, *Chicken Soup For The Prisoner's Soul*, another version of the Original Chicken Soup For The Soul, by Jack Canfield and Mark Victor Hansen. (To see my story online visit his website at: **http://www.angelfire.com/del/lagana)**

I have been blessed with the opportunity to earn a living speaking, so it is my responsibility, as a human being on this earth, to speak to those who need it, and cannot afford it. The story is as follows:

Pass It On

When I first began volunteering my services to the inmates at The Cook County Dept. of Corrections in Chicago, I was very hesitant. My hesitancy was not because of the caliber of the inmates (those accused of the most horrid crimes: murder, drugs, rape, etc.) but because it was not a PAID contract. Others I knew had paid contracts and I wanted the same. I thought to myself, "The state has plenty of money, so why should I speak for free?

I had a real challenge with that because I felt as though my services were being taken for granted. As a part time Radio Personality, I was always doing community service presentations, and here was an institution that could afford me, and was trying to take advantage of me.

As I took the time to meditate and think things through, I thought to myself, "Who am I doing this for, the audience or myself?"

After listening to my inner voice, I decided to go ahead and do it anyway, because I needed the practice, and I knew I had a captive audience, who could use some inspiration and direction. I also knew that n-o-t-h-i-n-g happens in this Universe without reciprocity. I would be blessed for sharing my time and talent, and that is what drives me.

After the initial visit, I was thrilled to see that these men, the downtrodden of society were so eager to learn a different way of thinking. One in particular comes to mind. A young man who had been there for the second time around who was quite adept at playing games with the minds of newcomers, such as myself, was so manipulative and cunning, it was unbelievable. At first I thought he was serious because he was always on time, the first to comment in class, or try and calm the fellows down when they began to get rowdy. After I learned of his background, I became cautious of him, and began to let the others have more speaking opportunities.

During one session, he was humbled by another inmate who `rarely spoke. This second young man was a gang leader and had no intention of doing anything other than what he was doing that landed him in the institution in the first place. The conversation was so startling, (I can't print it, but use your imagination, and you'd probably be right on target) I couldn't believe my ears!

Now this second young man was no prince, but I could tell from his conversation to the first young man, that he had been touched by something I had said during the course of "THE PASSION PRINCIPLES" techniques shared in class.

He said some things that you would not expect to hear from someone, who had no value on his life, or anyone else's for that matter. I would sometimes wonder if I was getting through to some of the men, but now I knew. If you treat people like human beings, despite their circumstances, some will act accordingly.

Both men were shipped out of that location downstate to a federal prison, but they left as men. They entered the county facility as boys with an attitude of anger and resentment, but left as men who were responsible for their own attitudes and behavior. They were learning how not to let he institution run their thinking, stripping them of the only true power they had, and that they were more free than those that held them behind bars.

They left empowered, knowing that the situation was only temporary, realizing that they had been blessed with an opportunity to develop themselves, and turn their lives around. That alone, was enough compensation for me. Knowing that I had made a difference in somebody's life, that had given up. Many of those who initially started the class, have gone onto other institutions or been released. I am honored to know that
they will take what theyhave learned, and to quote Patti LaBelle, "Pass It On."."

Passing it on is what I continue to do, whether they like it or not. You may think to yourself, well who wouldn't want to hear an empowering, positive, uplifting message? It might surprise you to find out who. No. Not the inmates, but some of the officers who guard them. It's not necessary to give names.

What is necessary, is that those individuals become aware of the power that they possess, and not abuse it. Power to control the lives of those incarcerated, is an awesome responsibility.

An officer downstate, shared with me how glad he was that he never mistreated or spoke ill to any of the inmates. At a later date he was incarcerated for a short period of time for domestic abuse. Before he even arrived at the institution, the word was out that he had been arrested. Word had spread to the alleged leaders of the gangs, not to let anyone disrespect him. It is alleged that many inmates are violated physically, as well as sexually, shortly after arrival. Fortunately this officer's arrival was welcomed. I am told, that most are not that lucky.

It all goes back to how you treat people. You can be in power one day, and stripped of it the next. I remember this same officer telling me how powerless he felt upon entering a jail, where he once told people what to do. Now it was the other way around. Now, that's food for thought. But not everyone thinks that way. Many of the officers and higher ranking officials in my training sessions at the Cook County Department of Corrections Officer Training, don't agree. A sergeant explained to me that they have been trained to view the inmates as animals, and to treat them accordingly.

We wouldn't animal rights activists just love this analogy? He adds that many have committed such hideous, unspeakable crimes, and deserve any and every cruel punishment, allowed by law. That may be true, but they are still human beings. They are even more than that.

They are spiritual beings, having an awful, human experience. Period. The real problem is that they are so far gone, they don't even realize that they have greatness within themselves. Another by far greater injustice, is that those who govern them (officers) on a daily basis, are sometimes not much better than those that they keep behind bars.

I only wish that they all remember the law of karma. What goes around, comes around. It's easier to pass on a blessing, than it is to block one.

Cornell McClellan
Owner of Naturally Fit
Personal Training Facility

Although he's a certified Personal Trainer and Martial Arts Instructor, McClellan's first passion is working with children. His twenty five year commitment to helping children, is a testament to that. Working with a community based organization for children, who are involved in the court system and might otherwise be incarcerated, is one of his greatest achievements. As a child he grew up observing men in the neighborhood go astray. He even wanted to be a gang member, like many of the men he saw. But with guidance from his parents, he was directed into a lifestyle that helps others improve the quality of their lives, not only physically, but spiritually as well.

Despite his reluctance, his hobby of teaching marital arts, blossomed into a career as a Personal Trainer. Even at the tender age of 18, it was evident that the Creator had a different plan in mind. Wanting to do more than just help people get in shape. McClellan says, " It means more to me than to just watch a person build muscle or fit into a smaller dress size. I want to help provide a balance, encourage them to look within and learn to use the heart and soul, as well as the mind.

It's much more than physical strength, it's all the elements combined that provides the ignition for the physical fire, which helps to strengthen the internal force. That is why it was necessary to a have place of my own, and not just a gym, but a facility that would allow me to incorporate those elements in my business.

A core obstacle for McClellan in this venture was funding for the project and a seller who believed in his vision. Locating an uncontested loop area, accessible from the north and south, with ample room for lockers, showers, parking facilities and public transportation for clients was a major concern. It's easier to start an entertainment establishment, than it is a health facility.

One of the lessons that I've learned that Cornell says that he can pass on to anyone in any field, is that it doesn't matter what business you're in, (real estate, social work or fitness) one still needs to have balance. Try to maintain integrity and surround yourself with people who will empower you, and help you keep focused.

It does you no good if you're a great businessman, but have unhealthy relationships. Finding a balance that makes you a great businessman, husband, father, and friend, is much more important in the long run, because otherwise it will eventually shows up as disease in the body. If you're not in tune with God, your health, and your family, everything else is in vain. Balance is essential. With everything you do, think clearly about it, leave your ego out and seek the truth.

As he continues to spread the truth, I am honored to have been one of his clients. I look forward to returning to the gym, to get back the body I left with, before I went on vacation. Every time I see Bonnie, (Bonnie DeShong, Radio Personality, V103) I am inspired to give it one more try. Bonnie has had her ups and downs, but she's hanging in there, and looking great! Continue to pass it on. It can only come back to you, *pressed down, shaken together, and running over!* Remember, don't become stagnant and try to hold on to it. Be the channel that you were meant to be, and let it flow through you.

Irene Valentine
Owner, Audio Word
South Africa

Irene Valentine, entrepreneur and Managing Director of Audio Word, an international organization that specializes in Secretarial Conferences in South Africa, is a testament to what can happen, once you make up your mind to do something. She and her husband owned several businesses together, including a country hotel, a conference centre, and one of two world renown African Carnivore' Restaurants. The partnership facilitated her personal growth, but the neglect of their personal relationship, and of their Christian Commitment, caused the demise of their marriage.

Their split resulted in him taking ownership of the hospitality and restaurant companies, and Irene took on the training business. Her short term concept was to fix the business and sell it, but the Universe had a different plan for her. Irene's struggle of course, was to see this change in her life as positive instead of negative. She had always wanted to be in an position to be able to help people, and this was a chance to do just that. Instead of seeing her staff, a team of twelve, as a noose around her neck during the transition, she had a paradigm shift and saw this as an opportunity to influence people, and make a difference in the quality of their lives. She views her team, as one of her greatest assets. We must learn to value people for who they are as human beings, not for what they do. We should be about restoring people.

That's what we're about in South Africa, restoring people and restoring grace. Irene offers this advice to anyone: "To see change as an opportunity, and not to worry. We don't worry about the sun coming up in the morning, or the moon's presence at night, so why worry about things over which we have no control? Change is the natural order of the universe. In the famous words of Jesus, Do Not Worry.......Is life not more than food? If it works for the sun and the moon, surely it will work for us."

I am honored to be a part of an organization, that has a leader, who thinks as Irene does. Many high ranking authorities don't value their employees, but that is not the case here. I look forward to her invitation to be the keynote speaker at the 1999 International Secretaries Conference, in Johannesburg, South Africa, and surrounding continents. It will be an event to remember.

Margaret Gatuhi
PEMTON, Ltd.
Export, Import Trading Agency
Nairobi, Kenya

During my visit to Nairobi Kenya last year, I was blessed with the opportunity to meet a young woman named Margaret Gatuhi, who graciously took us to some places that most tourists don't get the opportunity to see. We even got a chance to visit her lovely home. She and her husband made us feel so very, very welcome.

Margaret is a woman of moderate wealth, but was not born of royalty. She was born in a rural area on the slopes of mount Kenya 40 years ago, during the Mau Mau rebellion. There was a state of emergency as the local people resisted colonial rule from the British. The local people were put in small villages. About five families lived in one house, (a round hut, made of and grass) approximately 8 meters in diameter. It is under such circumstances that she was born, the fifth in a family of five, three sisters and two brothers. Due to lack of adequate health care, one of her younger brothers died before he was two years old.

In 1963 Kenya got independence and there was land consolidation. Before the emergency, people owned pieces of land scattered all over. With land consolidation the pieces were put together where people could build their own homes and do some farming, both subsistence and cash crops. In 1964 Margaret started school at age six. In a mission school built at the same place where she was born.

She completed her primary, secondary, and high school studies and she went on to Nairobi University, where she earned a bachelor degree, majoring in Economics and

Geography. She worked in the public sector for eight years, and for the last nine years she has worked for a multinational company. Margaret says, "I was most inspired by my mother who always told me to work diligently in school and become economically independent. She always said that if you have to beg for your needs, your hand will develop a curve. My parents did everything to support me in school, given the limited resources they had. I worked hard (at school and on our farm)to live a better life."

The challenges and obstacles Margaret incurred were especially tough during her teenage years since she had to resist a lot of peer pressure, like getting married. Margaret says that she did not like being in relationships with men who did not think education was important for a woman, or that schooling was not good for her. Her parents did a lot talking, telling her that she was the only one who could decide her future. She would decide her own future by the decisions she made during her formative years. She adds, "Therefore, I had to say no to men, who said they loved me, but who did not want me to have an education.

That was not easy. I did not want to give my love out of apathy and thus live their life. I postponed committed relationships until later years. I also got a lot support from my teachers in the mission school, who treated us as if we were their own children. The Christian morals we were taught, helped me tremendously. Parents and guardians always want their children to live a better life than they did. Sometimes the way parents express themselves to their children, can have a positive or a negative effect. Parents don't want their children to make the mistakes they made in their youth.

In many cases, successful people are successful because at one point they faced a crisis, and obstacle or a challenge, and were forced to make certain decisions. Therefore, when the going gets hard, double the effort in handling it. There is always a way to cross a river even for those who can't swim." Margaret adds, Your success is your own making, irrespective of your past. The riches of the world are meant to be yours.

Whatever your background, race, or family status, the future is governed by the decision you make today. Thus, bury the past, and don't let chains keep you from the future you desire. Look at life in all dimensions and see what a blessing you are to the universe.

Margaret's passion for what she does is evident in the life she lives. She is an entrepreneur, of Gatuhi Imports and Exports. If she can rise above the circumstances into which she was born, in Africa, surely anyone in America, can rise above their circumstances. Margaret sums it all up, in one phrase. She says, "My passion is who I AM, and what I do." From our short time spent together, I witnessed her generosity, and humbleness. My Kenyan has much to be proud of, despite her circumstances. Can you say the same?

Henry E. Ford
Author, Motivational Speaker
Twinsburg, Ohio

Named after the founder of one of America's favorite cars, Author and Speaker, Henry E. Ford, exemplifies what determination, and hard work will do for you. A man whose story resembles that of Les Brown, who was also labeled as mentally inept, Henry has proved them all wrong. Henry has taken the label assigned to him by aptitude tests and made a mockery of it.

Not only is he a successful businessman but his second career as a writer and speaker, continues to flourish. Henry feels it's his responsibility to share his story and his gift for gab with those who have been told that they cannot succeed. He says, "The best rewards I have found in this life involve helping those who are committed to productive and peaceful coexistence with others.

My experience has taught me that when an individual feels competent, committed and cared about by others, they perform with a degree of excellence far beyond what they and others believed possible. The gratification I feel being a part of the personal and professional growth of others inspires me to spread positive experience through my writing and public speaking."

Like anyone pursuing worthy goals, the challenges are many, but the rewards are great. The major task is making myself believe in the purpose and power God granted me. Most people in general, and I think African Americans in particular, have expectations of themselves several levels below that which they are capable of. I've learned that each of us is endowed without the potential for greatness. What we do with that potential determines our quality of life, and the ripple effect of how we live our lives affects generations yet unborn.

Ford tells everyone that they should "Find something that you love to do, and do it with passion and purpose. Continue to seek education, higher levels of competence and a deep commitment toward your chosen craft. Develop and nurture positive associations that support and supplement the beliefs that inspire you. The relationships you develop will return to you rewards in proportion to what you've invested. Reach to that higher power in your life for the power needed to sustain you during the rough times and energize you during the good times." Henry leaves us with this simple thought: "There is no shortage of resources in the universe. All of what you need, and much of what you want can be yours if you believe that success is you and then act in accordance with that belief."

It's apparent that Henry believes in himself. He started his second career as a speaker and writer, after the age of forty, when many think that life begins to go downhill. His first book, *Success Is You*, came shortly after he attended Les Brown's Speaking for a Living Seminar, and followed up with his second book, The Power of Association: Success Through Volunteerism and Positive Associations. He has a catalog of books, pamphlets, and a newsletter. He's a popular speaker in the Ohio area and travels extensively. Henry E. Ford, is truly The Communicator.

A communicator he is. Before the completion of my book, he was kind and generous enough to share with me invaluable tips on publishing my first book. He may never know how much I appreciate his confidence, his expertise, and his willingness to share. This is the stuff, great leaders are made of. I only hope to be a leader of such magnitude, arriving in the next millennium. People are precious. Henry is one of those precious people.

If you ever meet this man, you will know he's been touched by an angel. His wings are his ever present smile and his halo are his message. If you're ever in Ohio, give him a call. If he's not available, leave a message, and guess what? As powerful and important as he is, he will call you back. Maybe that's one of the reasons why he earned the title, *The Communicator*.

Michele S. Kurlander
Attorney At Law
Lindenbaum Coffman Kurlander & Brisky
President - Chicago Chapter of NAWBO
National Association of Women Business Owners

The responsibilities of motherhood alone are enough, but the added responsibility of being a professional, a chapter president of a major national organization, and a business owner, is quite an accomplishment for any woman. Michele is just that kind of woman, who takes on the responsibility of making things work. Like the diversity sessions she encourages members to participate in, as part of Chicago NAWBO's continued effort to involve women of color. These cultural diversity sessions were designed to bring together women of diverse cultures, discussing issues that confront women of all ethnicity, as business owners, and to help all women in business work together to speak with a strong, combined voice in challenging government and Corporate America to revise the antiquated rolls and level the business playing field.

Her role as president of the second largest of NAWBO's 72 chapters, is evidence of her efforts to assist corporate culture in understanding women in business. She joined as a member in 1988, working on a variety of projects and chairing a committee. Ten years later she is still striving to make a difference in the lives of women business owners. She travels to the nation's capital to lobby for issues that affect NAWBO members and works closely with other organizations in such efforts. Her greatest venture does not come from the legal matters in her work as an attorney in a law firm, in which she is one of four equal partners, and the only woman. Her greatest formidable task is as president of Chicago NAWBO, working for the organization's issues, including its efforts to expand it's membership.

Michelle says, "It's very exciting to see this organization grow, and see members from all different types of industries and all size business sizes participate in this process. It has really grown sincc I joined ten years ago." Michele has grown with the group from being a member in 1988 to being a president chapter in 1997. She continues to make a difference in a world where the old boy network still reigns. With the power Michele Kurlander packs, she continues to work continually at bulldozing the barriers erected to prevent women from obtaining the same business opportunities allowed to their male counterparts. Though the journey may be long and arduous, she has learned a very important lesson along the way. ***Breaking stereotypical attitudes toward women takes time.*** A proven process is to tackle one person, one step at a time. Look out Corporate America, there's a new president in town. Michelle is headed your way to alert you to the benefits of having a woman business owner on board.

Bother Spade
Multi Media Artist

Inspired by God to utilize his talents, Brother Spade clearly states, "Working as an artist is the sum total of everything I've done up until now." He's been blessed to have been able to work in many different types of industry, including the fashion world as a model, athlete, actor, and recording artist.

Having been blessed with so much is sometimes a challenge. Spade expresses, "With all of these things not fully blossoming, I needed to direct my energies elsewhere. So I quiet myself a lot with prayer and meditation. Of the many things that I do, they require money up front. I had to do something that doesn't require an immediate outlay of cash. A good example is when I was working as an artist in the music industry. It cost money to produce a demo, and to shop it around. My demo tape had not gotten to the right people, so it didn't catch on. I needed to focus on utilizing my raw talent, that doesn't require that.

His brother Warp, also a talented artist, introduced him to sandstone, (which is meticulously carved stone derived from

sand) and using that medium brought profitability. Once we achieve success in the sandstone business, the finances will be available for us to complete our other projects." The sandstone business is flourishing. The two brothers travel throughout the United States showcasing their art, and have been featured on many television shows, including The Oprah Winfrey Show.

Spade credits his success to the drug addiction he overcame nine years ago. As a cocaine dealer and user, he was involved in various illegal activities which eventually ended in imprisonment. He credits his time spent incarcerated with having the time to discover and nurture his true talents.
His foremost obstacle has been discovering the difference in knowing, and believing the truth about his true identity. He

knows that he is a child of God, but circumstances will appear that cause you to doubt yourself. He says, "We don't know if it's really working or not, and sometimes it's hard to keep practicing the truth." Despite appearances, he knows the difference between realizing, believing, and knowing God.

"It's always a challenge to get beyond what I have been told, and to be quiet and listen to what he has to say. If you really want something in life, you have to keep going, you cant stop just because you have problems. You must experience all the ramifications of the challenge. After taking the time to quiet yourself and listen to your inner voice, you come to a realization that success becomes yours, and not an image of what the world or the mirror tells you.

You must go through whatever it takes to get you to the point where you want to be. You must go through the experience, there's no way around it. Like a man who's made up his mind, determined to handle any storm that come his way. Spade concludes, "In whatever you do, Put the Father First."

Brother Spade is a prime example of someone who has talent, but early on was misled and used his talents in a destructive manner. It is by the grace of God that learned how to harness and distribute that talent in a positive and constructive way. He is indeed a role model for those who say it can't be done. Sometimes we must go the long route to get to our destination. M.C. Richards says, "There is no substitute for putting one foot in front of the other." Where will your greatness lead you?

Jacquie Haselrig
Program Director WGCI-AM 1390
Radio Personality/WGCI-AM 107.5

Her daydreams as a young person were filled with her being in front of an audience. Jacquie Haselrig, Program Director of WGCI-AM 1390 and Sunday morning host on WGCI-FM 107.5, searched for a career that she could have fun with and fulfill her desires to perform. She didn't know how to get from point A, to point B, to point C, as a singer. Her aspirations as a singer were unduly discouraged by Finis

Henderson, Jr., a friend of her father's, who was working for Sammy Davis, Jr. He told her, point blank, that singers were *a dime a dozen*. But that didn't stop her.

Jacquie came to Chicago from Johnstown, Pennsylvania, doing what she had to stay active and what she enjoyed the most, which was theater and music. She got involved in musical theater in Hyde Park. Jacquie continued taking voice lessons and singing on the weekends at little bistros in the Rush Street area, where there were piano bars. This was all before her son Miles was born.

While working for the United Negro College Fund, where she'd worked for almost two years, she decided that she wanted something more out of life. She wasn't sure what it was, but she knew she didn't want to be a secretary the rest of her life. Not that there was anything wrong with it, she just wasn't good at it. She had to find something exciting to do. She had friends in radio and she thought if they could do it, so could she. She already had a good speaking voice. She definitely wanted to do something fun, so she decided on a career in radio, something easy, or so she thought.

She decided to go to school for radio, something she thought would be fairly easy and quick. She took a course in radio. She obtained her FCC license, (which was a requirement then, but since deregulation, it's not required anymore.) but still couldn't get a job, because she had no experience. So she went back to school, this time to Columbia College, which was then located right off Lake Shore Drive. Jacquie says, "Every time I went back to school, I got a job."

She got her first radio job as a disk jockey on WJNL, a 50,000 watts station, and WJNL- FM an easy listening station, in her home town of Johnstown, Pennsylvania. Continuing in the entertainment field was a must for Jacquie. In radio, she could continue to perform, and not have to take any major risks.

Being a female, in a male dominated industry was an experience. She was fired from a job, under the disguise of not knowing how to do the news, which she was not hired to do. Also, because of her allegiance to a Program Director, she was passed over for a promotion for a midday show slot. Often times she was passed over for a promotion, where the job was given to a male who had less experience.

Moving back to Chicago in 1977, to WBEE 1570, a Jazz format radio station, Jacquie subsequently joined WGCI in August of 1981. Another scenario that she constantly faces is being in a managerial position with co-workers, who are now her employees. Not being second guessed on decisions is another battle. It's part of the old boy network.

Jacquie has learned that if you treat those whom you manage with respect and understanding, they will give the same back to you. It's important that you keep an even temper at all times, and if you need to vent, do it behind closed doors. You can't let the people that you supervise see you as being weak.

She advises anyone in this industry, from her interns, producers, to those whom she takes the time to teach, " To believe in yourself first. If you believe it, you can achieve it. Believe in God." She's constantly telling those just starting in radio to learn everything they can. What they learn from her and what they may learn on their own, puts them in a better position in this industry. Jacquie says Gospel Singer Vicky Winans complimented her on how real she was, a real down to earth person. This 17 year veteran of radio humbly admits that, "I can be real because I don't have any hidden agendas. This is my job, and I am not trying to get over on anyone. I do my job, and I do it well." Indeed she does.

She's the only female Program Director in a major market in the Chicagoland area, on Chicago's number one urban station, keeping Chicago's All Dusties 1390 on the top. As The Queen of Sunday Morning Gospel continues her ministry of music, Jacquie has earned everything she's gotten by hard work, persistence and patience.

Dr. Vietta L. Johnson
Director of Orthopedic Surgery
Provident Hospital

Unless you have a foot or ankle problem, you probably don't think much about an Orthopedic Specialist. Vietta Johnson, is a young woman who makes the difference in the lives of many of her patients.

Dr. Johnson, was initially inspired to become a physician, by a very simple method. It was simply a calculated, analytical deduction. She says, " I attended a Science and Math High School. Since I liked people, and I was science and math oriented, I figured it out. People plus science and math equals physician." She had a girlfriend who was in a special program for minorities and suggested that she get in it too, so she did. It was a medical program for students interested in medicine, taught by medical students. They took science courses on Saturdays for about two and a half years, and classes that exposed them to medical school life, physicians, etc. Dr. Johnson says with the same joy she expressed the day she joined the program, saying, "I loved it." She had found her niche.

Moving on to college, she studied pre med. She took the basic requirements, a year of calculus, a year of biology, a year of inorganic chemistry, a year of organic chemistry, and a year of physics. Then you could declare any major that you wanted. But she took a very circuitous route to orthopedics. She got talked out of it initially because she was interested in sports medicine. In doing research for sports medicine she found out that 70 percent of athletic injuries, which is known as soft tissue, or *non operative* injuries. She then figured she could be a Physiatrist, which is a Rehab doctor, who does physical medicine and rehabilitation.

When she left med school, orthopedics was her first choice for residency but she had gotten brainwashed into thinking she wouldn't make it in that field. Vietta was told she had to be number one in her class; she had to know everybody, and she'd have to do tons of research. She admits, "I even brainwashed myself into thinking I couldn't. I told myself that I couldn't do surgery because the mask made me feel claustrophobic and I couldn't breath. So I convinced myself that I wanted to get some sleep and have a reasonable lifestyle. Working as a Physiatrist, their workload is light and a less hurried lifestyle. It also occurred to me that I couldn't complete my patients care if they required surgery. As a Physiatrist, I couldn't help them if surgery was necessary."

If she did go into sports medicine as a Physiatrist, a great deal of knowledge she had acquired, she was learning from orthopedic surgery. So if she had the opportunity to be a orthopedic surgeon, why wouldn't she be one? As a orthopedic surgeon she would have the option to perform surgery, but as a Physiatrist, it would not be an option. Vietta wanted to have as many options as she could, in order to provide full care and service. s things turned out Dr. Johnson's professional journey took her down long roads with many winding turns.

She even did what's called a *transitional residency*, which means she went through many different services. She did internal medicine and general surgery, and then she got to choose. She even did an extra month of rehab because she wanted to see what it was like at that particular hospital.
Dr. Johnson laughingly says "I was bored out of my face. I literally told myself that I couldn't justify paying back my medical loan. She then did a month of orthopedics, simply loving every minute of it, having a great time. She loved it, and the hospital staff liked her as well.

The time came to make a decision on what hospital she will choose to complete her residency. There's a process called the *match*. This *matching* process is when you rank what hospital you want to go to for your residency, and they rank you. She knew that since she was already at the hospital, they were going to rank her high enough to stay there and work. In order for her to remain in the matching process, she had to go through the her medical school, which was Harvard. The hospital had openings in the orthopedic department. The reputation Vietta had earned, and the rapport she had built would surely help her land the position. The hospital asked her to apply and she did. But things didn't go as well as anticipated. Dr. Johnson says, " When people really don't want you to have something, they try and block you, but ultimately if God has something in store for you, it will happen anyway."

The field of orthopedics was then, and still is, dominated by Caucasian, men. These doctors had little experience and no interest in focusing on *matching* women, especially women of color. Dr. Johnson was not matched with the hospital that she chose. She adds, " I think I am about to match in ortho, and then staff ask me what happened, because I didn't get the match?" Vietta indicated that she took the necessary route, and she had only matched with one hospital. That hospital was the same one she was doing her residency at, so she didn't know why she didn't match, because it was the only one she applied for.

She was so disappointed after they told her that her name didn't show up on the *match* list. She is sure that Someone conveniently didn't put her *match* number on the list, because they wanted her to stay in rehab, and not go into Orthopedics. Ortho has very few spots, and a whole lot of people want them. If you rank them as number one, and they rank you as twenty one, you might not get that one. So the hospital that she was really interested in thought she was playing around, that she wasn't serious about working there. As it turned out, they discovered it was a computer error. Ironically, as God would have it, the guy who did *match,* turned the spot down because his wife refused to raise her children in New York City. She was then offered the position, and accepted.

Despite the temporary setbacks, Dr. Johnson was the first black person to do a residency at New York City, St. Vincent's Hospital. "I literally went through hell, with gasoline drawers on. It took years after that residency for me to convince myself that I was worthy of what I had attained." After reading the following incident that Dr. Johnson shared with me, you will probably understand why she felt that way.

When Vietta was rotating in orthopedics, the chief resident asked her to meet him downstairs in the emergency room. Upon arriving outside the emergency room door, he started yelling at her swearing, "I don't even know why you're here. Women have no place in orthopedics. Women are essentially fun to play with. Otherwise, you have no business here?

Most of the Chief Residents viewpoint was based on experience with a woman who previously worked there. The previous woman had used her feminine mystic to gain and maintain her lifestyle. With all kinds of thoughts running through her head, Dr. Johnson says, "I am thinking to myself, that this guy is going to be my Chief Resident. He runs my schedule; he tells me which cases I can go to. He has a lot of control of my daily schedule, and he thinks I shouldn't even be here?

As things would go, Vietta happened to be dating an attorney at that time, who instructed here to document everything, and she did. She was accused of many different things including ignoring answering her pages though she was on call and working 60 hour shifts. Her voice rises as she shares another incident. "I even had a hamburger thrown across the room at me by the Chief Resident. This man was so loud in voicing his anger towards me, that the nurses had to come out and ask him to be quiet because he was disturbing the patients. It got so bad, that the staff even told him point blank, to *quit torturing me*. After putting up with both physical and mental abuse, I eventually had to go to talk to my chairman, in my second year.

I informed him of what was going on and had it well documented. I told him that I would no longer accept this man's abuse, and that the next time he insulted me, I would serve the Chief Resident the next day with a letter from my attorney, requesting that he restore professionalism to that department. If he didn't adhere to my wishes, I would take him to court. I told him in no uncertain terms that too many people in my family had worked too hard for me to get where I am.

My mother picked cotton and my grandmother still worked at white folks houses, and I'd be damned if he was going get rid of me. I have been to the great ivory institutions of the country, if not the world. I went to Princeton undergraduate school, and Harvard Medical School, and I'm coming here for this? I would not leave. If I go, everybody in here will go." I will shut this place down." She left the chairman standing there with the letter in his hand. It's sad to say, but as far as I know, in 1993, I was the first and only black female to graduate from a surgical program from that hospital, and the institution has been standing since 1879. There was one other woman who studied there but left after two years.

One of the lessons I've learned from the experience is that the resident chief that I had all the negative encounters with, knew very little about women and black women in particular.

His experience with women was with the one who came before me and the little he did now about black people was from what he saw on television.

This Chief Resident couldn't even understand why people would call Vietta Miss, instead of Doctor. So she invited him to go on rounds with her. He was astounded at the patients and staff who wouldn't address her by her title. Even though she was dressed in full garb, lab coat, stethoscope around her neck, proper identification, Vietta had earned the right to be called doctor. Certain people would not give her that respect.

White patients would walk pass the white nurses, and go to the back where she sat writing on patient charts, and ask her to dump a bed pan. She notes, "Not that it was beneath me to empty a bed pan, because I would do it. But just don't take for granted that because I am the only black face sitting behind a nurses station, that I am there to empty your bedpan." It's sad that the majority of people just don't know, or don't take the time to learn about black people.

Ironically this same resident chief who challenged her from day one, sent word by one of his staff to New York. He had entered private practice and wanted Vietta to enter into a partnership with him. He knew that she was a hard worker and got the job done. She was still in her third year of residency in New York and he had moved down to Florida. No way was she going to Florida. But at least they came to an understanding. He shared that he was also discriminated against because he was Italian, coming from a poor family, and all the negativity associated with that.

Dr. Johnson has chosen to rise above the obstacles set before her. She currently spends her time divided between two hospitals: The historic predominately black Provident hospital in Chicago, and she also holds a faculty appointment at Loyola. Additionally, Dr. Johnson is Medical Director at the wound care center at St. Margaret's Mercy Hospital in Hammond Indiana.

Dr. Johnson has a word to the wise for those interested in medicine. "Know that medicine is truly what you want to do. Most important, you must love people, as I do love my patients. I play music in my clinics to ease the tension from patients." This young doctor who will be receiving the 1998 Kizzy Award says, " One of my goals is to make sure that the two brothers who came into the orthopaedic residency after me will never have to endure the torture that I experienced. I have kept that promise to them." That's the sign of a pioneer, making sure that a path is cleared for others to follow.

Hats off to Vietta L. Johnson, who has earned the right to be called doctor. For all of those patients who refused to acknowledge your credentials, we thank you for your continued contribution, **DOCTOR** Vietta L. Johnson

I cannot express enough the importance of networking or joining trade organizations in your industry. It was through meeting Helen Montgomery, Public Relations Director of Lexicor IS, at a Saturday morning networking event, that I met her boss, Renee Franque. Ms. Franque needed a voice over artist for her voicemail system. Helen knew me not only as a business owner, but she also knew that I host a radio show. As a result of becoming a member of the Chicago Chapter of NAWBO, (The National Association of Women Business owners) I not only found a new client, but developed new business relationships. This next entrepreneur, is a talented young businesswoman, whose bound to be listed as an upcoming Fortune 500 company.

Rene Franque
Owner
Lexicor IS

A hard worker, with a good work ethic, and a strong background in sales, Rene Franque was bound to become an entrepreneur in the Information Technology field. Rene says she knew there was a lot of opportunity in this arena , and it was ripe for entrepreneurs.

Her 15 years background in IT sales, and a good sense of customer commitment made her realize that she could make it on her own. Renee says, "I knew that I could make a good living on my own as well as for somebody else. I wanted the freedom that comes with being an entrepreneur, and there were a lot of opportunities financially and career wise."

Her undergraduate degree in Computer Sciences and a masters from Northwestern, prepared her for the business. One of the many challenges new business owner face is the support of the infrastructure, such as rent, overhead, support people, etc.

She has learned along the way when it comes to bidding on projects, not to bid too low, and really understand the value of her services. In addition to being business savvy, Renee says, "I have to take my time in hiring good people. The best advice she give for entrepreneurs is solid. She says, "Do good planning in the beginning make sure you have a well written business plan first. Have all of your ducks in a row, so you can carefully embark upon a new venture instead of reacting. For those interested in venturing out there on their own, Renee leaves us with the words of a true entrepreneur, someone willing to take a chance. Renee says, " The sky is the limit!" This is true spirit of an entrepreneur. Ms. Francque is part of a growing breed that is definitely headed in the direction, where she will determine how high her glass ceiling will go. Can you say the same?

You've heard the American Express commercial, "Success has its rewards". So does failure. Sometimes it necessary for us to fall before we realize that we need to do something other than what we are doing at present. It's all part of the growth process. Oftentimes it's necessary that we become dissatisfied with where we are in life before we decide to do something about it. Dissatisfaction is often a blessing in disguise. This next story is a testament.

Mary Mitchell
Columnist
Chicago Sun-Times

It would probably surprise many people that Mary's desire to become a writer was not out of inspiration, but out of necessity. Mary says, "I really became a writer to save myself from a life of bitterness and discontent. I never lived up to my potential. Not through elementary, high school, my personal life, my job, or career. I just never pushed myself. I was the kind of person who was content to be good looking and have a good time, just surviving. Once you go through that phase in your life and you come out of that you realize that you've just wasted a lot of your life. You realize that you haven't lived up to your mission, whatever the reason that you were put here on this earth. You discover that you really haven't' done it. That's a scary thought."

Mary realized very late in life that she needed a college degree. She also needed to prove to herself that she could get one. She goes on to say, " I needed a college degree to prove to others, like employers and those kinds of people who had one, that it wasn't a private club. Anybody could belong as long as they fulfilled the requirements."

As a present to herself for her 40th birthday, she looked at where she was in life and decided that she wanted something more. She knew she could do better. She says she looked at her life and said, "This is not it. This not what I want to be for the rest of my life. I was a legal secretary, and I thought I could do better than that. I am by no means knocking the profession, I just wanted something more than secretarial responsibilities (making coffee and making someone else look good.) I thought there was something else I was supposed to do and I wasn't in the right place doing it."

What's interesting is that for twelve or thirteen years she worked for a law firm right across the street from the Chicago Sun-Times Newspaper where she currently works. Mary laughs as she adds, "So that meant for all those years I was going to a place full of discontent, full of unhappiness, and constantly being denied a raise or a promotion. They discriminated against me for twelve years, and all along, right across the street was really where I was supposed to be."

Blessed with the good fortune of having an instructor at Columbia College who recognized her ability, he encouraged Mary to apply for a scholarship at the Sun-Times. He told her that an internship was something she needed and that he thought she would do very well. At the time, Professor Bednarski was an Editor at the Chicago Sun-Times, but has moved on to Crain's Electronic Media. It just goes to show that if you're really serious about making a change in your life, the Universe will provide you with the necessary resources.

Instead of partying over the holiday weekend with everyone else, Mary took the time to prepare for what would one day enable her to become one of Chicago's finest journalists. It's ironic that the deadline for applications was on a holiday. She used her time over that Memorial Day weekend to her advantage. She skipped the picnic and all the other festivities and stayed home. She wrote her resume, cover letter and the required essay. She hand delivered it to the security desk in the lobby of The Chicago Sun-Times, informing the officer that she was applying for a scholarship. Talk about stepping out on faith.

Mary says, "I think I got the internship because they were impressed that I had enough nerve to even apply. I had no writing background, had never worked on a school newspaper and had never written a deadline or any of that. Mary Dudinski, managing editor at that time, probably felt that if they didn't give me the opportunity, then no one else would. That 's how I got in. The summer of 1990 I interned with five other people. Mary goes on to say, "I was very discouraged because I was the least prepared of all of them because I had no prior experience. The very first day I couldn't even think. I stuttered. I couldn't talk. I couldn't do anything."

She made it through despite the odds. She survived. She got a break, and that's really all it takes *if you prepare yourself* for what you really want in life. She worked with a lot of people who helped her learn the business. She broke stories and worked harder than a lot of people. She didn't mind rewriting a story over and over to get it right. She wasn't embarrassed because she didn't get it right the first, second, third, fourth or sometimes fifth time. She wrote it until she got it right. She was willing to write it over as many times as it took. She knew it would pay off. Eventually it did. At the end of the summer in 1990, they offered her a part-time job. She had just graduated from college. Getting a job at a major newspaper is unheard of in the newspaper industry. (I know this to be true because I tried. Thank God I didn't get hired. I probably never would have started writing for myself.) She was the first Columbia graduate they had hired in a long time.

Mary says it never crossed her mind that she wanted to become a writer to impress people. She admits that she didn't even have a writers spirit. She says, "I knew I could write, put a subject, object and verb in a sentence. I always enjoyed poetry which I have gotten away from now. I started writing as a kid because there was nothing else to do. I had a l lot of sisters and brothers, and we would get together and write plays. We would take our socks and scribble eyes on them giving them a face, pretending they were the characters."

She always knew that she was good at writing, but having been out of school for so long, she took the easy courses like poetry and fiction writing. Mary says, " When you're going back to school after all those years at the age of forty, you don't want to become a biology major." Naturally she took courses that appealed to her. She adds, "I am a reader, I read everything."

One of her biggest challenges is trying to maintain a spiritual balance. She hesitates before saying, "Journalism is a medium that is somewhat of a Godless field. It is humanistic as opposed to a spiritual field. People do not share spirituality, except for the religious right. After God had brought me to that point in my life, and I believed that it was ordained that I am where I am, I realized that I was neglecting my spiritual base. It has been a challenge to remain spiritually focused. In this business, you develop a writers mind, and in the media you develop a reporters mind of skepticism and you just begin to doubt. You can have a very good career on the outside, but it doesn't mean that you're happy on the inside. People sometimes end up killing themselves. You think to yourself, God I thought that person was so happy. Some people look like they have a great life and their spiritual and personal life stinks. I have not always been able to maintain that balance, and sometimes I do it better than other times. I know that it is because of the humanistic field that I'm in."

When Mary first started in the business she was active in church, she attended Sunday School and church on a regular basis. She even sang in the choir. It only took a couple of years for her to drift away from that. One of the reasons was because of the pressure of having to work all different kinds of schedules. Sunday became a day of work as opposed to a day when you pray, In this business you also develop a hardness about yourself, because if you don't people will take advantage of you. Mary openly admits, "I was just not doing the things I needed to do to maintain my spirituality. You might be the kind of person who doesn't need to go to church, but you might need to pray. If you stop praying, you're in trouble. That's the kind of challenge that I experienced."

I can personally attest to the fact that this is just one of the challenges that people in the media experience. If you don't have a sense of your true self, you will get lost in all the glitter. Success does come with a price. Pausing, Mary said, "People that *knew me when*, marvel at my success. I always say what good does it profit a man to gain the world and he lose his soul? That is what I have to remember. That is the lesson that I have learned through all of this. I learned this throughout my career, from the people I report on and in my personal life. I even got divorced while I was in this business. It was not easy having to start over with my family. I saw the impact that it had on my children. It was tough watching them go through that process. I am lucky that I remarried. I married a great man who is good to me, but I must confess that divorce was not a good thing to happen. I have learned is that there has to be a balance in everything, it's only a job. Somebody else's picture will be running in that space when I am dead and gone."

She's finally gotten it together. This year was the first time in eight years that she took a vacation, and did not work. In the past, she's always left some work, sent some work, or did some work. She has always had some work with her while on vacation. But this time she didn't. Mary says, "Now I turn off when I come home from work. I spend quality time with my children, and I take very few assignments on the weekend. I give time to my relationship with my husband. The paper is a great career. I love my career and I love what I do, but it is only a part of my life, not my whole life."

Mary laughs at this one herself saying, "It's hard to be married to me. I'm public, high profile, and outspoken among all those things. My ex-husband went to Columbia and also studied journalism, but his career never took off. When I look back on it, why wouldn't he feel bad? Wouldn't it be a challenge for him to become Mr. Mary Johnson? My husband teases me about how we will go someplace sometimes and people refer to him as *Mister* Mary Mitchell, and it's a joke. But he's very comfortable where he is."

Sometimes you are thrust in a career where things happen very quickly. Things happened to Mary very rapidly and being able to handle it is an awesome responsibility. Mary had the same thing then as she has now. She had a house, children, a husband and responsibilities. Mary says, "I didn't have that footloose fancy free life where you are Miss Reporter and it's all about you. I never had that. So I had to balance the public part of me with the private part of me, and my personal life suffered until I learned how to do it. I had to go throughout the process of hard knocks and hard feelings, falling down, being stressed out too much, making mistakes, neglecting my family life. I tend to be a workaholic anyway. I had to see that this is what happens as a result."

Mary leaves us with a word from the wise. "Find a balance in life. Bad habits are easy to creep up on you in this business. Learn how to handle your relationships, job, children and school. The media is made to seem so glamorous, and a lot of it is. I know that I would not have met half, most, no I dare to say all of the people I've met, had I not gotten into this business. But you only have one family, and they grow up so quickly. There are some choices that you make, and one of those is to be true to yourself. Take care of yourself because that's' the only way you're going to be able to do the best job you can do as a journalist."

Mary continues to take care of herself, her family, and the community in which she serves. She provides a balance in a newspaper that does not cater to the needs of the African American Community. Mary Johnson Mitchell, woman, writer, mother, wife, and community activist. A living legend in her own time, making a difference.

The so called *problems* of life usually appear to teach us lessons. When we stop to listen to what the experience is trying to tell us, that is what makes the difference between getting the lesson this time around, or repeating it again. Sometimes life has to lay us flat on our back, before we get the lesson.

This young lady used what many would see as a setback, as a comeback. A life threatening illness can be a devastating experience, but was used instead to turn a small business, into a million dollar empire. That empire is headed by Michele Hoskins.

Michele Hoskins
Michele Foods, Inc.
Calumet City, IL.

What really inspired Michele, is that she wanted to be independent. She says, "If you really want to be successful on a business level, you should probably think about owning your own business. I was teaching school, and I had three daughters, but I wanted more than that." She was going through some challenges, and wasn't quite sure of what she wanted to do, so she asked God to send her something to do. Michelle says, she is very, very spiritual, and placed her faith in God, who gave her the vision. She was going through a period where she was reading a lot of inspirational books, and she got the vision to become an entrepreneur.

Michele says "An entrepreneur is something inside of you, it's not something you can just pick up on. First of all, you have to have a lot of *faith in yourself* because you're not going to have a lot of people who have faith in you. Because when you come up with a plan or an idea, and it's your own personal plan, no one is going to co-sign that. They see that as your thing, and if they help you with your thing, your thing might be successful, and they don't have a thing. So an entrepreneur has to be someone who has a tremendous amount of faith in themselves."

She couldn't get a loan from anyone for her vision, because she was not bankable. She chuckles as she adds, "I was just like anybody else, living from paycheck to paycheck, I didn't have a lot of credit, I didn't have a home, I didn't really have anything. And what I did have, I had to sell to get to the position of even looking like I was worth any bank risking giving me a loan. So I sold everything that I owned. I was going through a divorce. My husband and I were separating. I had a condo that I kept because I had children. I had furniture, furs and things I had accumulated over a period of fifteen years. I liquidated it all, selling everything I owned and moved back home to my mom's attic, with my three young daughters. I decided to market a recipe that my great Great Great Grandmother had handed down to me from three generations."

Michele says, this recipe, was the same recipe her Great Great Grandmother used as a slave to cook for her slavemasters. The reason why she decided to market product is because it is unique, and marketable. She always tell people that they have to have a product that is marketable, you don't want to reinvent the wheel. It has to be something very unique, and very different. After she researched the market, she discovered that there was nothing else like her Honey Cream Syrup available. So she went through a process of learning how to sell her product in the market. She had no cash flow. The only thing she had was faith in herself. Michele found a company, called Resources, that helped entrepreneurs who had unique recipes, whose product had to be marketable. She had to submit her proposal, and out of 350 applicants, they chose her product.

This company had the expertise, but she had to come up with the capital. That's when she went through the process of selling everything she owned, coming up with a total of $150,000.00 over a period of maybe nine months. After that nine months, she had a product that was formulated by a chemist. and a graphic designer for her labels. Michele found bottles,, caps, and someone who could make her syrup in a fifty-five gallon drum. With the patience of Job, she hand filled the bottles in the basement of her moms house, after getting off work from her part-time job. She had quit her teaching job and was working part time for Mr. John H. Johnson, at Johnson Publishing Company, as a makeup artist for Fashion Fair. She would fill bottles in the evening, and on the weekends take them around to local grocery stores, and put the product on the shelf. She told the merchant that if the product sold, she would come back in thirty days and invoice them, And if it didn't sell, she would take them off the shelf and they would never have to see her again. She says she sent twelve people in to get the product off the shelf. That's how she had to do it.

After six months and forty eight grocery stores, the product started selling itself. At that point, she was still hand filling orders in the basement. She went to a fancy food show in Atlanta, Georgia, and at that point Michelle says, "I realized who I was. Who I was, was an African American woman in the food business. I was the only one, because there weren't any others. I also realized that my syrup was a general market product, it was not ethnic, and that I was in the upper scale market. I realized that from the response that I got, when receiving 350 orders. I went back home trying to fill those orders by hand, realizing that this was not making me any money. I realized that this was not the way to do this business." She had to find another way.

She made an appointment, and went to Jewels Food Stores corporate office in Melrose Park. With confidence in her voice, she spoke with a buyer whom she demanded that the thirteen key stores in the African American community stock her product. With a more serious tone she adds, "If he didn't give me what I was asking for, I was prepared to *get black* on him. Armed with persistence and naiveté, Michele did not know the rules of the grocery game. She didn't know that they wouldn't accept products prepared from a basement. She had to have a full scale operation in order for them to place an order with her. The buyer said he would give her general market space. He also said that he had been in the business for thirty-five years and he'd never had a minority that had anything to sell to Jewels. (Had he never heard of Famous Amos cookies?)

He literally put her product in the stores and gave her an order for six-hundred and seventy two cases. She was a bit dismayed because she wasn't prepared for such a huge order the first time around. She was thinking to herself, "How was I going to do this? It took me an hour to fill one case."

Michele found a packer who helped her move producing the syrup out of the basement, into a packing house. The co-packer said she had enough orders for him to make it for her, and she delivered to Jewels in twenty-one days. The first invoice was for sixteen thousand dollars, it cost her fifteen thousand to make. That's literally how she started in business.

From there Michele went to Dominick's, another grocery store chain, which resulted in her obtaining eighty percent of the Chicagoland market. After paying a co-packer to package and deliver it, she was hardly making any money because she didn't know anything about pricing. She hadn't priced syrup products: she was just making syrup and selling it. After about a year she decided she had to get serious. She started learning about procurement and many different aspects of the business, including how to buy her own raw materials.

It took her about six or seven years to figure that out. She stayed in the Chicagoland market. After nine years of struggling, not having any office and still working out of her mom's basement, she had gone from middle class to low income, and was on welfare.

Michele says without shame "I had to make sure my children could eat. I was no longer working for anyone because Mr. Johnson fired me because of conflict of interest because he found out I was in business for myself, he thought I was competing against him. He taught me what a salesperson was and he even commended me for doing such a great job. I was very competitive and wanted to have the best quota every month, but I wanted to sell more than color. I wanted to sell skin treatment. I did my research on skin scare and started treating women's faces. I knew a lot about skin care, and since I was a teacher, I got very good at what I did. I was making his counter at Marshall Fields forty five hundred dollars a week and become the top sales person. He came to me and wanted to give me a better position, involving traveling. I told him I couldn't because I worked for myself, so he told me "You're fired." I told him, fine." He literally did the best thing that someone could do for an entrepreneur, and that action on his part put me into my own business, full time. Today, I still thank him. Whenever I see him we even laugh about it."

From that point on, Michele worked full time in Michele Foods, trying to figure out how to pay rent and all kinds of other crazy stuff that goes along with being in business for yourself. She still had no structure, no bank loan, no staff, just out there putting product on the shelf whenever the stores needed an order. Thing just were not going in the direction Michele wanted. It was time for her to get serious and make some money. Michele decided to go national. She wrote a business plan, very basic, to show that if she sold a case per week in X amount of stores, it would generate a thousand, ten thousand, 50 thousand, 100 thousand, million, dollars, etc., as she grew nationally with this product. She showed lenders how se would do in store demonstrations, sell the product with discount coupons, and different things she had leaned just by observing and researching, and studying the business.

Michele shopped around at many different banks, to no avail. She had no collateral and the business wasn't doing great; it was still a risk. Eventually, she found an investor, whom she calls her *angel*. A black minister introduced her to him by telephone. She dropped her business plan off at one of his offices on her way home one day from Melrose Park. He showed his investment bankers who agreed it was a great investment for him. Not only she was an African American woman with a good product, but had survived nine years, had good accounts, and was already established in major grocery chains. The business wasn't making any money, but it showed consistency.

The investor angel gave her a line of credit for $150,000, and in 18 months she paid him back and had taken the company from zero to a million dollars. She did it by going national. She took the product to eleven divisions of Kroger Supermarkets, and everyday was on a plane traveling to another state to market her product. She basically focused on the South, even selling to the Winn Dixie chain.

She would meet with a buyer, get the sale, place an order and ship the cases in. She gets very serious at this point saying, "I tell this to people because this is a very important part of who I am what I've done, because this is where God came back in very, very strongly. I started out on faith with God in this, because God is my partner, and he was with me every step of the way.

In 1992 after receiving this money from this investor, and taking the product national, I started getting very bad headaches. I was not able to see, and as I traveled, things were getting progressively worse, to the point where I actually could not see. I could see shadows, but that was it. I could see you coming towards me, but I couldn't tell if you were male or female. I couldn't see if you had black hair or anything, because I couldn't see color."

Michele thought that it was simply an overload of stress and even attributed it to *going through the change,* because she was 44 years old. All the doctors all told her something different. One doctor said it was stress from running a company. Another said it was because she didn't have any money, or because she didn't' have a man. Everybody was giving her a different scenario. It got to the point where Michele was taking Motrin, Prosaic, and every kind of painkiller she could get. She even began taking acupuncture weekly, and visited a chiropractor. She went to her minister and he would anoint her with oil, praying on her head. Just doing all kinds of stuff, but none of them worked. This went on for nine months.

In the ninth month, her doctor called her and suggested she go to a headache specialist, which she did. She took a test called the MRI, and a tumor was found on her pituitary gland that was very, very large. It was pushing on her visual nerve. They gave her six weeks to live. The doctor said it had to be removed immediately.

In retrospect, Michele says, "The tumor was actually a blessing in disguise. What it did for my business was provide me with a fresh new business perspective. Although I had been in business for nine years, I had no power of attorney: no 401K plan: no structure: no will: no nothing. I was just out here selling. So what God was saying was, let's get some structure here. The way to do that is to sit you down and confine you, and make you lay on your back. And the only thing that could lay me down was a tumor. Nothing else could do it. Not even excruciating, blinding headaches. I had went through all this pain, and I was still working, still traveling, going through airports with magnifying glasses, trying to see. I had to squint my eyes and wait for someone to get real close to me before I could see who they were. I had my daughter reading menus for me, reading my contracts, driving me around, etc. I was still functioning. The only thing that could stop me was laying me flat on my back."

Her surgery was scheduled for the upcoming Thursday. There was a neurology convention coming to town that day and some of the world's renown Neurologists would be there. So she met with another specialist, and rescheduled surgery for 5:30 am the following Tuesday morning. They warned her that there was no guarantee, and they didn't know what they would find in her head because it had been there for such a long time. She was afraid at first, but with reassurance from her *angels* along the way, she went into surgery, knowing that she would come out, just fine.

Michele takes a breath and says, "One lady in particular assured me after praying me, that the surgery would be a success. She assured me, that the strength God would pull me through. I shared with her that I was so afraid, and she prayed with me. Before I went under, I had a talk with God, and realized that this was just another challenge. If you're spiritual, you can understand that. After that, I knew that I was going to come out of it. I prayed and released the fear. I had become very peaceful before the surgery. When the surgeons opened her head, they found that the infection had immediately spread throughout her entire body. They thought they had lost her. By the grace of God, she lived to share this experience.

Out of that experience, she has a renewed sense of business. She even went back to see the lady who had prayed with her before surgery, but her office had moved. She knew she had been one of her angels, as they were all around her, all the time. She also knew that God was preparing her to share her story.

Some time had lapsed after her surgery, but Michele was able to get back to running the business. About a year and a half later, she was at it again, this time calling Denny's every Monday at 10am. Michele laughs as she shares this next entrepreneurial tip. "I had called so much, so consistently, they knew me by name. I was very adamant about getting this account, and I did, to the tune of four million dollars. It literally changed the face of my business, taking it to a whole new level. We now had cash flow. We were able to support the retail operation. We are able to do more things and this resulted in us getting a lot of publicity. I started getting requests from the Sun-Times, Black Enterprise, and many others." I know this to be true, because I met Michele at the 1998 Women's Business Development Conference, and it took me a while to even get up close to her, to try and get this interview for the book.

Michele goes on to say that, "I looked at the retail market and decided to go after General Mills. A friend of mine at South Shore Bank, and I, had discussed this about 4 years ago. Well I signed the contract in September of 1998. The buyer said he was amazed at my persistence. I tell people al the time that persistence is part of what an entrepreneur is. It's just like being born with blue eyes and blonde hair, or being born with black skin and brown eyes. Entrepreneurs have certain qualities, and persistence is one of them. Just like endurance, and belief in yourself, are other characteristics, persistence is just a natural function of what I am. If I go after something, it has to not be good for me, not to get it.

General Mills was a perfect example of what a company needed to do. I convinced them that it was the right thing to do. African Americans spend money just like everyone else does. General Mills knew this to be true and invested in my product. They're about to kick off a really big campaign with radio and television. They're getting ready to put Michele's syrup as the syrup of choice with Bisquick, and the slogan is, *Let's make a better pancake*.

Despite seemingly insurmountable odds, standing in line as a public aid recipient with 3 small children, to buy her own syrup with foods stamps, Michele knows it can be done. There have been obstacles but they were also blessings. She has always known that with the help of God and faith in herself, she can do anything.

Michele says, " I am blessed with being an African American woman, who's been in business for 15 years, who can sit down and share with other African American women who don't know what to do. It goes to show that you don't have to go the traditional route and have all the things that they say you're supposed to have. I tell people all the time, do not concentrate on money, because money is not the answer. The issue is you. What is your vision and what do you want to do? Whatever it is, just get up and do it. Nike-size!

I am positive this is why God gave me this blessing to share with other people that regardless of where you come from, or where you are, you can get to where you want to be. It's like when I did the Oprah Winfrey Show, people say that it's been a long time, but it hasn't been, because we're in the now moment. Something is always happening now, to prove tomorrow."

African American women need to be able to look at her story and reap the benefits. When she started out there were few mentoring programs, or women owned companies. Now we have doors open to us, whereas we didn't have them before. Michele notes, I had to kick and knock down doors and persuade people I was a good risk, and persuade people to put stock on the retail shelf, despite the fact though I couldn't pay the stock charges. Now there are all kinds of ways to get help. I thank God for all the blessings. I am thankful for the recipe given to me by my Great Great Grandmother who told me, *don't just keep passing it on: make something out of it.* So in addition to passing my daughters the recipe, I will pass a business on to them. Wherever they go in life, they always have something to come back to. I will continue to give them the support and security they need to be strong women."

A strong African American woman Michele Hoskins is. She didn't let anything get in her way, including blindness, so don't anything stop you. With God as your partner, how can you fail? The next time you feel like giving up, pull out a bottle of Michele's Honey Cream Syrup, and make it a great pancake day!

We don't always know immediately what the next step is in life. We simply need to be open to suggestion. Michele is a good example of that, as is Iyanla Vanzant. While on tour promoting her latest book *In The Meantime*, she revealed to me during a radio interview that she stopped practicing law in 1991, but wasn't sure what she would do next. What she did know to do immediately was to get quiet. She had to spend some time being still in order to hear what the next move was for her to take. Iyanla said, "When you get rid of one thing, you make room for the something else. I just realized that law was not where I was supposed to be. When I realized that, so I just stopped. We think that when we leave one job we have to immediately go out and find another one. Sometimes we just need to get clear about what the next job should be. We need to get clear on what it is that we need to do, and what did we learn from our last experience."

She admits that it took her a while before she went out and started doing anything. For a long time, she didn't know what she was going to do, then things just began to unfold. People began to approach her. She didn't go out and seek the work, people went to her and asked her if she would do it.

The path is always laid out in front of you if you're paying attention, you can follow the signs. Iyanla adds, "In the meantime was getting clear and working through the fears, and the self limiting beliefs that keep you from doing the stuff that you need to do, just trying to hear what Spirit wanted me to do." She admits she had reservations about doing what she was guided to do. We 're always wondering if we're on it, if we're doing the right thing, if you're doing it well enough. You always worry about that, as long as you are human, you're going to have that issue.

As strange as it may sound, Iyanla says sometimes she still doesn't know if she's on the right path. She laughingly says, " Whenever it turns, I turn, when it goes up, I go up. When it goes down, I go down. Its not about right or wrong, it's about doing what you can, where you are, with what you have. Right now, this is what I can do. This is what brings me peace, what brings me joy, and if I get a new direction, I'll follow that one."

We're often afraid to follow new directions because of what others might think or say about us. This last, but not least story, is from a young man who has gone way beyond the limits of what was expected from him and made an empire.

Barry Mayo
MayoMedia

Results are what made this next young man, the millionaire that he is today. This radio Mongol, turned photographer, is a legend in his own time. People in the radio industry know him as none other, than Barry Mayo. What people don't know about this man, is that the same passion that drove him to become the General Manager and owner of Chicago's Best Variety of Hits and Dusties, V103, (102.7 FM) is the same passion that drives him today. (and keeps him in the darkroom of his new found love, photography, until the wee hours of the morning)

The Genesis of Barry Mayo's interest in radio goes back to when he was around five years old. He loved music. One day Barry's father brought home an old RCA Victorola and a box of 45 rpm records. (This was before the days of audio cassettes and CD's. At that time, you either played 45's or an album, or a reel, which only the elite could afford) Barry would take his dad's box of records, and select a few to hear. He stacked them neatly, all on top of each other, placing them carefully, so that the arm of the music box, would play them one by one.

It was in elementary school that Barry developed an interest in science. He began building radios and transmitters, which led to exploring and listening to all kinds of music. From the third grade Barry attended all white schools while still living in the ghetto. He wisely took advantage of the exposure to dual cultures.

Following his graduation from high school, Barry attended CUNY for two and a half semesters before dropping out. The next time he tried his hand at going to college Barry chose Howard University, where he studied radio. He was a few years older than most of the students and possessed easily recognizable leadership qualities, the latter being confirmed by his peers, who elected him as General Manager of Howard's student radio station WHBC. Barry does admit to being a "horrible disc jockey"; is was in programming that he found his niche.

Dean Barrow of Howard, mistakenly thought Barry was a senior. The dean informed Barry of a job opportunity in Little Rock Arkansas for a Program Director. Not only was Barry "called", he was also chosen. Despite phenomenal odds, Mayo says, "If someone was crazy enough to me a job as a Program Director, and I'm still a junior in college, then I should be crazy enough to take them up on it." Of course, you know how the rest of the story. Barry once again becomes a college dropout.

Twenty-one years would go by before Barry would tackle college for the third time and complete a degree at Columbia College, graduating in 1997. To fully chronicle all of Barry's endeavors during this time would require rewriting a separate book. (Never know, perhaps it will be my next project.) Between his stints at CUNY and Howard, Barry was bitten by the entrepreneurial bug. He read the book, Think and Grow Rich, by Napoleon Hill and bought into it hook, line and sinker.

Suffice it to say that Barry has gotten and made breaks for himself in his radio career be it in the Big Apple or Second City or stops in between. Everything he touched, has turned to gold. There has never been more than a six month period of unemployment for Barry in the radio business.

From small steps to giant leaps, Barry successfully negotiated the move from programming to management to ownership. Again, he got by with a little help from his associates and friends. IN this instance it was Lee Simonson who prodded him to move from Program Director to General Manager, and eventually to radio station owner. Lee's sage advice to Barry was "If you're interested in radio, you already have the reputation of being the top Black Program Director in the United States, and if you can run KISS FM for four years without messing it up, you will be able to get money from any bank you want. Very few people in our industry (radio) are good at both sales and management.

While Lee was General Manager at WOR and Barry was General Manager at KISS FM, they went to some venture capital firms to get money to start a company. They found an investment banking firm called Morgan Louis Githens and Ahn which provide 15 million dollars to start Broadcast Partners, Inc. BPI, the company bought five radio stations; one of those was WBMX. Barry moved back to Chicago to run V103, and oversee the programming for all five of the radio stations. As General Manager of WBMX focusing on the daily responsibilities of operating a number one radio station, caused the job to lose its luster.

Barry says, "I was not happy in management. My last three years at BPI I was not happy because my first love was in programming, the creative side of radio that moved the masses to listen to radio in the first place. In the end it became an issue of cash low, budged, profit and loss. Mastery was achieved, but I wasn't passionate about it. In 1993 when we went public, I was not happy inside when we sold the company. Aside from the financial aspect of it, I was really bored and miserable, and didn't even know it. I took the summer off and then I started consulting.

Each step of the way has its own set of challenges: marriage, divorce, parenting, therapy, None as challenging as being married, which ended up in divorce. One of the greatest challenges for business people, is to be, and stay married, and raise children. Although my marriage didn't work out, I still have a fantastic relationship with my children's mother, and my children.

Of all the challenges I have had in all my life, family is what's most important. Raising children is what its all about. That's it. Business opportunities come and go. You'll work at one place for so long, and you leave. Soon to be forgotten. Relationships and your children are forever. I'm a single dad, with a sixteen year old son who lives with me. I've got a thirteen year old girl and eight year old son who lives with their mom, and her new husband, and I'm cool with them all. That's important, because any static that's between the parents, affects the children."

Barry makes an excellent point. He continues to serve as a leader in the community, and part of that leadership consists of sitting on the board of Providence St. Mel, as he has for the past nine years, helping our future leaders of America realize their own potential.

As a consultant, companies pay his company, Mayo Media, for his advice on doing things he's done for a long time. He feels good about that. Barry says, he feels exactly like he did in 1978 when he first got started in radio." I belie that the principles that helped propel my success in radio, are totally applicable in this new venture. He humbly says that he plans to have the same success in photography, that he's had in radio. Barry says, " I Would say to anybody, besides reading Think and Grow Rich, To Thine Ownself be true. You really have to think about what's important. Get excited about something. When you talk to people about business and success, you don't hear them talk about being excited a lot.

Very rarely do you back into real success. The fact of the matter is, something happens, and you get excited about. Anything that you get truly excited about, you will do well at it. You will do well, because it's all you think about. After my kids, I now eat, sleep, and live photography. If you come into my room, it is literally filled with photo magazines and stuff like that. I was the same way with radio back in the 70's. I couldn't get enough of information. So I have no choice but to do well, because this is all I am consumed with. And of course we all know, that which the mind can conceive, and believe, it can achieve. The thought of failure has never even occurred to me. I'm to excited about this!

For the first time in 10 years, photography has given me the creative outlet, that radio once gave me. Photography is like music. It's the same thing, I hear it. I play music while I am in the darkroom. I have not been this excited, this alive in many years. It gives me the opportunity to exercise my creativity. The action is where the music is. Like the O'Jays said, I Love Music!

What's happening with the radio business with consolidation and deregulation has taken all the joy out of it. Competition is different now. One company owns most of the station in one format. If I was at V103, would they really want me to kill WGCI? Of course not, they own both.. I could not have gotten out of the local radio station market at a better time. Radio is run and owned by publicly traded companies. The reason d'etre is all about financial growth, cash flow, margins, *not* the types of things that turned me on to the industry.

So you're got to do whatever it takes to make money for the station. If that means firing a bunch of people, (if you're missing your revenue numbers) or not spending the amount of money you normally spend to market and promote yourself, (because you're not hitting your budget, you do it, no questions asked.) Or in a programming sense, moving two radio stations away from each other, when in fact the best radio for the listeners would have them compete and hit head to head with each other. That's all backwards to me. But it's all fine. Radio is making a lot of money, it's worth a lot more than it was back in the old days. I have turned down more jobs than I care to tell you about, because I don't want to be a part of that process. It takes me away from the experimental, the creativity element.

Photography allows me that creativity. I am going to try to not let anybody or anything to get me off course, because I never wanted to be a GM. It worked out fine, but it certainly took me away from my passion. I will never do something like that for money again.

After you make a certain amount of money, and you can pay your bills, and buy your toys, what does it mean to have more? Life really isn't about having lots of money. Its about living from a state of passion.

Throughout the course of interviewing Barry, I've begun to understand just what makes him tick. Being passionate about the people and things that matter the most. Things and people that get, and keep him excited about being alive. Be on the lookout for the next Gordon Parks Jr., Coming soon to an art gallery near you, with the best variety of images and silhouettes. Barry Mayo is truly a renaissance man, a legend in his own time, living his life, as we should all strive to live ours. On fire, with Passion!

All of the people in the preceding stories are from ordinary people are just like you. All trials and tribulations have a common thread, the challenge to make you grow. The essence of these stories contains the truth. That truth is, no matter what you've been told, there is more greatness within in you than you will probably ever realize. Just when you think you've gone and done your best, there's more that awaits you. In the words of Dr. Winston Johnson, "Do your best until your best gets better, and your best and is yet to come.

So don't settle for less. (Which doesn't always mean money.) There is so much more to you than you can ever imagine. Your imagination can take you wherever in life you so desire. Once you achieve your desired goals, don't forget who you are. Your greatness envelopes so much more than what the human eye can focus on. In the words of Oprah Winfrey, 'Unless you choose to do great things with it, it makes no difference how much you are rewarded, or how much power you have." So use your time, your talents, and your energy wisely.

"A job pays the rent
training for a vocation, provides you with a career
your passion is the journey,
in which your purpose unfolds."

Take a long, deep breath, and continue the journey. Keep your passion alive!

Recommended Reading

Acts of Faith
In The Meantime
In The Spirit of Man
One Day My Soul Just Opened Up
Value In The Valley ....Iyanla Vanzant

A Course in Love............................Joan Gattuso

A Course In Miracles......................Foundation For
Inner Peace

Chicken Soup for The Soul
Chicken Soup for The Prisoner's Soul....Jack Canfield
(see Zelda's Story) Mark Victor Hansen

Daily Motivations For African Americans
What Makes The Great Great!
Think & Grow Rich: A Black Choice
Wisdom of The Ages............... Dr. Dennis Kimbro

Do What You Love,
The Money Will Follow...................Marsha Sinetar

God Is My Broker.........................Christopher Tyler

Heal Your Life...............................Louise L. Hay

How To Let God Help You.............. Myrtle Filmore

If Those Who Reach, Could Touch..........Mac Donald

It Ain't Over Until I Win
Live Your Dreams..............................Les Brown

It Only Takes a Minute
To Change Your Life!........................ Willie Jolley

Lessons In Living......................... Susan L. Taylor

Lessons in Truth...............................Emily Cady

Living In The Light.........................Shakti Gawain

Love Gone Wrong
Wisdom For The Soul .... Toni Turner

Minding The Body, Mending The Mind.......Bory Senko

Mutant Message............................ Marlo Morgan

Open Your Mind and
Be Healed......................... Dr. Johnnie Coleman

Return To Love....................Marianne Williamson

See You At The Top............................Zig Ziglar

Spiritual Economics.....................Eric Butterworth

The Lady, Her Lover,
and Her Lord..................................T.D. Jakes

The Holy Bible.....................Whatever Version Spirit
reveals to you to read

The Holy Koran....................The American Version

The Holy Qur'an......................Islamic Original Text

The Peak To Peek Principle...............Robert Schuller

The Power of Association:
Success Through Volunteerism Positive Associations
Success Is You............................ Henry E. Ford

The Science of Mind..................... Ernest Holmes

The Seven Spiritual Laws of Success... Depok Chopra

7 Habits of Highly
Effective People........................... Stephen Covey

Daily Inspiration For Better Living............Universal
Foundation For Better Living
(312)568-2282

Science Of Mind Magazine 1-800-256-1984

Creative Thought........................1-800-662-1348

Dial Inspiration...........................(312) 642-4449
Ext. 11

INDEX

About The author

Zelda Robinson, **CEO, of Zelda Robinson Communications**, is an ***International*** **Speaker/Training Consultant.** ZRC specializes in **Career/Personal Development and Teen Mentor Training.**

A graduate of Columbia College, in Broadcast Communications /Photojournalism, her speaking career is a spin-off of her part time passion as a Radio Personality. She began her radio career at **WNUA 95.5 Smooth Jazz**, and now hosts Sunday Mornings on **WGCI-AM 1390, Music of Love & Inspiration. She is a certified Trainer in Career & Personal Development, Crisis Counseling, and teaches at Truman College in Chicago.** Her speaking has taken her around the world, from **London, England, to Nairobi, Kenya, East Africa**. She'll be touring with the International Secretaries Conference in June 1999 in Johannesburg, **South Africa**.

Among her clients are **Motorola, Commonwealth Edison, Cook County Department of Corrections, The Center For Urban Ministry, and The Mayor's Office of Employment & Training.** She is a member of **The National Speakers Association, Professional Speakers of Illinois, The National *African American* Speakers Association in which she is Publicity Chair, The American Society of Training & Development, Association of Women Journalists, UNIFEM, The Chicago Association of Black Journalists, the American Association of University Women, as an advisory council member, and is a board member of Goodwill Industries, In.** She has been featured on **WGN's Channel 9,** *Minority Entrepreneur of the Week*.

Zelda's passion has taken her life to the next level, and her mission is to take the masses with her. Whether it's on the air, or at a live presentation, the message is still the same. It doesn't matter where you come from, what does matter is where you're going. Take yourself, or your organization into the next millennium with **Zelda Robinson Communications.**

Need A Speaker? Personal Life Coach?
Top leaders and winner have one.
Why shouldn't you?

The greatest leaders, athletes, entertainers, alike have personal coaches. Michael Jordan has a coach. Les Brown has a coach. Kathleen Battle and Mariah Carey have a coach. All winners have someone to coach them. The top organizations have team leaders, so why shouldn't you?

People need encouragement and the proper skills to move them forward with their life plans. If you're in charge of being responsible for the training or motivating of staff, students, organizational members, I can help you with that process.

I bring a wealth of experience of someone who had little of anything and learned to make lemonade out of the lemons given to me. Your lemons in life, are simply a test of your willingness to squeeze the juice.

As a member of the National Speakers Association, Professional Speakers of Illinois, The American Society of Training and Development, member and Publicity Chairperson of The National African American Speakers Association, I bring with me a wealth of information, understanding, and willingness to help you connect with your purpose, power and passion.

If I cannot personally accommodate you, I will recommend a speaker in your city. Contact me today by phone, fax, email, or visit my website, to see how we can begin to address your needs. Looking forward to the possibilities.

Training
Seminars/Workshops

Business Category

The UPside of DOWNsizing

Speaking With Poise and Passion!

Networking Strategies, Do's & Taboo's

Crisis or Challenge, How To Handle Corporate Chaos

Job Readiness Workshops

Burning Bowl For Better Business

Interpersonal Communication Skills

Successfully Managing People
Through Coaching & Counseling
For Outstanding Performance

Time Management

Too Blessed To Be Stressed Workshop

Master Minding For The Next Millennium

The Passion Principles
(Finding your dream and following it!)

Creative Category

Purpose + Passion = Prosperity

Grieving, Growing, and Going On

Don't Just Earn A Living, Make A Life!

No One Ever Told You, Well Now You Know!

What's Love Got To Do With It?

What's God Got To Do With It?

The Laws of S.E.L.F. Esteem

How To Find Mr. Right
(and Keep Him)

Getting The Job You Want,
Making The Money You Want!

Need a fee quote?

Call (312) 642-4449

or visit our website at:
http://www.zeldaspeaks.com
email: zelda@zeldaspeaks,.com

Participants Praise for Zelda

"Our company is currently undergoing change, and Zelda's presentation rekindled our commitment to training."

-Mrs. Tami Brent
T & D Training Director
Commonweath Edison

"Your presence alone is powerful! Your message will reach the multitudes that you wont' reach through radio. You were have the power, use it!"

-Les Brown
The Motivator

"On behalf of the institute of Personnel Management, Kenya, I thank you very much...this will help our staff re-examine themselves..."

-A.G. Muteshi
Chairman- Kenya Institute of Management Personnel

"When Zelda speaks, her thoughts are compelling, researched, and entertaining."

-Art Norman
Anchor, WMAQ Channel 5 News
Former President, Chicago Assoication of Black Journalists

"I've been using the techniques you shared with us, which has made me more appreciative of just being. Thanks for helping me to help my staff."

-Sister Rose-Martin Glenn
Chicago Youth Centers

Benefits of Programs

The highest percentage were in the following areas:

- personal productivity
- build confidence and self-esteem
- develop better relationships at work and home
- less sensitive to others disapproval
- heightened sense of values
- less worry
- have more fun
- overcome fear
- gaining sense of peace

To Hear Daily *Inspiration*

Call The *Passion Principles* Inspirational Line

Dial (312) 642-4449

Press #11

We keep our Inspirational line local so that anyone who needs inspiration can have it, so they don't have to call a 900 number.

God Gives it to us freely, and freely we share our gifts.
Share this number with a friend, or someone in need of a lift.

Join The New Passion Principles
Personal Paradise Network

Excerpts taken from her best selling book, her daily MMM, (MasterMinding Messages) Zelda shares the importance of staying in touch with your inner self. Listening to the still small voice will give you the answers you need, and keep you on track with your true purpose, and alive with passion!

This network includes passionate people who are living their dreams, and sharing it with others. To keep your passion alive, you've got to read, listen, and attend events that serve your pupose. This network of people with similar interests gives you the benefit of the experiences of others with similar purpose.

PPPP Network Membership Benefits Include:

- Your story posted on Zelda's website (FREE Advertising!!!)
- Free email subscription to her daily MMM
- Quarterly Email Publication
- Access to the Passion Principles Inspirational Line
- Early Bird Availability and Discounts to ZRC Seminar/Events
- 10% off any book, cassette, upcoming seminar or workshop.

_____Yes, I would like to be a member of the Passion Principles Paradise Network. Annual dues $35.00

(PLEASE PRINT ALL INFORMATION REQUESTED)

Name ____
Phone (   )______________Ext. _______
Address____________________________________Apt./house_
City______________State__________________Zip__________
Email: ______________________ www ____________________
Form of payment ___Check/M.O. ____Visa ___Mastercard
Account Number_____________________Exp. Date_________
Cardholders Name___________________Signature__________

The Passion Principles *Paradise*™ Order Form
A Division of Zelda Robinson Communications
Make Checks Payable to:
Zelda Robinson Communications (312) 642-4449
P.O. BOX 118305
Chicago, Ill. 60611

Career/Personal Development Investment Products

Ship to Address

Name ______________________________
Phone (   )______________**Ext.** _______
Address ____________________________
City, State & Zip ____________________
Email: ____________________ **www** ________

Quantity	Description	Price	Total
ITEM # PPB	The Passion Principles, Pathways to Purpose, Power & Profit!	$20.00 *Personally Autographed*	
ITEM # PP-ASC	The Passion Principles Audio	$ 10.00	
ITEM # PP A6C	Passion Principle Live Radio Show	$59.95 6 Audio Cass.	
ITEM # NWS	Networking Strategies, Do's & Taboo's	$10.00	
ITEM # TTSPT	Top Ten Speaking Tips	$10.00	
ITEM # JUW	Getting The Job U Want, Making The $$ U Want!	$10.00	
ITEM # REP1	Earn Passive $$ Special Reports	$10.00	

Website: http://www.zeldaspeaks.com email: zelda@zeldaspeaks.com